NEED A LITTLE HELP?
Call me.

I'M HERE TO HELP

Stop banging your head against the wall!
The LSAT and law school admissions aren't as
mind-boggling as you think. If you're struggling
with a certain question type, or you're confused
by the whole "sufficient vs. necessary" thing, or
you want to know how to negotiate for law school
scholarships, please let me help! I'm a nerd about
this stuff, and I love to show students how easy it
can be. Email me any time at **nathan@foxlsat.com**,
or just pick up the phone. I'm generally available to
talk between 10 am and 6 pm PST.

STUDY SMARTER

Join me and my co-host of the Thinking LSAT
podcast, Ben Olson, for access to our killer
LSAT explanations at LSATDemon.com. The
Demon learns from your mistakes and gives you
questions targeted toward your weaknesses,
at your ideal difficulty level. Do timed sections
at 35, 53, or 70 minutes. Attend full proctored
practice tests with other Demon users around
the world. And do it all from anywhere—on your
phone, tablet, or computer.

Do a 7-day free trial today at **www.LSATdemon.com.**

No confusing jargon, no pulled punches, no bullshit.
LSAT made simple.

Copyright © 2019 by Nathan Fox

Design copyright © by Christopher Imlay

Layout and design by Eric Uhlich

Published by Avocado Books, Los Angeles, California

ISBN: 978-1-4802-1189-6

Introducing The LSAT:
The Fox
Quick & Dirty LSAT Primer

by Nathan Fox

Table of **Contents**

Prologue

As an LSAT teacher, I make my living from future lawyers. But, having been to law school myself, I'm skeptical of law school's value for many students, so I'm perfectly happy to talk you out of law school if you're not 100 percent sure. I'll sleep soundly knowing I saved you three years of your life and hundreds of thousands of dollars. Of course, if I can't talk you out of it, I'll do everything I can to help you crush the LSAT, get in to a solid school, and grab a scholarship while you're at it.

THE BAD NEWS

The typical law school sucker looks a lot like I did: I applied late in the application cycle, to just a couple schools. I should have applied more broadly, and I should have negotiated for a scholarship. At many schools, over half of the class gets scholarship money, so if you don't get one, you're essentially paying for your education and for someone else's.

When I started at UC Hastings in 2008, I had no plan for what I'd do with my degree when I graduated. I didn't personally know any lawyers and had no idea what lawyers really did. Once school started, I found the work epically boring. Oops! I skipped half my classes and spaced out on the Internet when I did attend.

Even without interest or much effort, I still passed all my exams. The school had no incentive to flunk me; it wanted my tuition. I worked through school to defray some costs, but three years later I graduated with $160,000 in debt and a monthly loan payment that was more than my rent—*in San Francisco*. And of course I never practiced law, because I was never meant to be a lawyer in the first place.

Even for people who find they do want to do some actual lawyering, law school is no guarantee. Tuitions have skyrocketed while bar passage rates languish below 50 percent at some schools. Students who manage to pass the bar struggle mightily to find well-paid work in legal practice. Some schools have been known to fudge their employment stats by counting waitressing or summer internships as "employed" when reporting their numbers. Jobs are so scarce that law firms, hiring for receptionist positions, routinely receive resumes that contain the letters "J.D." on them from hopefuls looking for a backdoor to the job they actually want.

New grads lucky enough to find actual legal work are often disappointed to find themselves endlessly reviewing documents, working 80-hour weeks, and toiling on corporate cases they don't find meaningful. They don't make as much money as they expected, either: They'd heard that the average new lawyer makes $80,000 a year, but this average is skewed by a very lucky few who make six figures right out of the gate. Most new lawyers make more like 50 or 60 grand. And that giant loan payment is due this month, and next month, and every month after that.

And if you fail the bar? Tough: You can't discharge your student debt through bankruptcy, so you'll owe this money forever, whether or not you practice law. Recently, some unemployed lawyers have tried suing their schools to recoup their

Don't Go To Law School
(But Get A Great LSAT Score If You Do)

tuitions. I suppose they're getting a chance to do some lawyering, but it's probably not what they intended when they started law school. (At least one of them lost their case, by the way—it ain't easy trying to sue an institution comprised entirely of lawyers.)

Depressed yet? Good. Lawyers need to see both sides of every case. If you're going to persist on this path, I want you to do it with your eyes wide open.

THE GOOD NEWS

A select few of you do know what lawyers do every day, and actually want to do that work. You're not here because you have a cockeyed fantasy that law school will make you rich; in fact, you know that it almost certainly won't. You're here because you want to change the world. You're not just Type A, you're Type AAA+++, and you literally won't be able to sleep at night until you're a real practicing lawyer. (And you're fine with not sleeping much once you become one, too.) If this is you, then you'll be a great one. And the good news is, for you, there's scarcely been a better time to apply.

As word has spread about law school's many problems, fewer and fewer people have applied. Applications have fallen a lot: The annual number of people taking the LSAT is down 50 percent from where it was a few years ago. That means it's a buyer's market for a J.D. who's ready to work. LSAT and GPA ranges are falling at even the top-ranked schools, which means that well-prepared students with strong numbers are getting into better schools *and* getting generous scholarships when they do.

So now that you know the realities of law school and what your life might look like when you're on the other side of three tough years, do you want to continue? If so, I have more good news for you: You've cracked open the right book. I'm about to show you how to crush every section of the LSAT and get started on that legal career you're after. If this is the right path for you, I'm ready to do all I can to help you out.

Welcome

Even the nastiest college dorm room can have the illusion of cleanliness with about 15 minutes of work. Toss out the beer cans and pizza boxes, give it a quick once-over with the vacuum, and you're ready to party. In about 20 percent of the time, you've got 80 percent of the job done. Sure, the remaining 20 percent of the job will require *much* more effort—if you want to get it *really* clean, in a manner that wouldn't disgust your mom, you're going to have to bust out the Clorox and waste your whole weekend. But getting that initial 80 percent done means you've made a huge dent in a very short time. That's exactly the purpose of this book.

In the pages that follow, I'll teach you 80 percent of everything you'll ever need to know about the test in far less than 20 percent of the time that a typical book or course would require. I'm not telling you that you don't have to work hard to achieve your LSAT goals. But I *am* telling you that this book will make the job a lot less painful.

No matter who you are, or where you're at in your LSAT prep, now is the perfect time to grab this book. Shockingly, a majority of students sit for the LSAT with no preparation whatsoever. If you do nothing more than read this book, you'll have an enormous advantage over most of your competition. If it's three days before your test, and you're pooping your pants, this is the book to read.

And if you're planning to embark on a longer study program—two months or longer is typical for most of my students—this is *still* the book you should read first. I give it to all my students on the first night of class. After all, if Mom is coming to town, you're going to start with the beer cans, right? Rather than banging your head against the wall, start here and let me take the pain out of the most common obstacles. If you like this book, and want more, you can move on to my other, longer volumes from here.

How to use this book

Read it cover to cover. Simple as that. Start with the Intentionally Blasphemous Ten Commandments, and then read through the sections on Logical Reasoning, Logic Games, and Reading Comprehension. In each section, I've given you one or two of each of the LSAT's most common types of questions. It won't take you more than a few hours, and it will be by far the most useful hours you'll ever spend preparing for this test. The last chapter will provide you with ideas for future study, if you're looking for more.

Meet your guide

I took the official LSAT in February 2007 and scored 179. Shortly after that, I began teaching LSAT classes for a well-known test prep company. After coming to the realization that I really loved teaching, I started Fox LSAT in the summer of 2009, between my first and second years of law school. And I've never looked back.

Which means that by purchasing this book, you're tapping into the benefits of almost a decade of daily LSAT practice. Here's what I do, in my tenth year as an LSAT teacher, to keep getting better:

Teach. My students are my best teachers, and I learn something new in every class. For ten years I've shamelessly pirated my students' best ideas and distributed them to successive students.

Write. I've recently released my sixth LSAT book, which is entirely devoted to the Logic Games. It was my most challenging book to write and edit, by far. Putting things down on paper crystallizes ideas and forces me to think about the test in new ways. You can find all of my books on Amazon, by the way.

Podcast. On the *Thinking LSAT Podcast*, my cohost Ben Olson (from Strategy Prep, based in Washington, D.C.) has continually pushed me to think about the test in new ways. I love hearing how Ben explains questions and teaches topics. I'm sure I interrupt and argue with him too much, but then again, I probably learn the most when we argue. If you're interested, you can listen in at www.thinkinglsat.com.

I welcome your feedback on this book. Please email nathan@foxlsat.com, or call or text 415-518-0630; that's my personal cell phone. And yes, I really will respond. I have the greatest gig in the world, and I wouldn't have it if it weren't for people like you, helping me get a little bit better every day.

Meet the LSAT

The Law School Admission test is an all-day examination offered at a minimum of four times per year. Scores are good for five years. If you take the test multiple times, law schools will see all your scores when you apply. However, most schools will only use your highest score to evaluate your candidacy.

The test consists of four scored sections: Two Logical Reasoning sections (short arguments), one Reading Comprehension section (long reading passages), and one Logic Games section (word puzzles). Each section has a strict 35-minute time limit. The test also includes an "Experimental" section and a handwritten Writing Sample, both of which are unscored. We won't waste time on those sections in this book— we'll just focus on the scored sections.

WHAT DOES THE LSAT TEST?

I believe that the LSAT tests three important skills, all of which are very relevant to your future career as a lawyer.

English language skills.
I won't sugarcoat this one: Lawyers in the United States are gladiators who do battle using the English language. If for any reason your command of English isn't strong, you're going to have a much tougher time convincing people that you're the gladiator they should hire to represent their interests. It might not be fair, but it's the truth.

The LSAT is, quite clearly, testing your ability to read and understand English at a fairly high level. I worry when I hear a student say something like "I'm not a big reader," because readers have a huge natural advantage here. Unfortunately, there's not a lot an LSAT teacher can do to help you with this part. You either grew up a reader, or you didn't. If you did, you're starting with a leg up.

Focus.
This one can be trained for. The LSAT presents you with dense, complex arguments, puzzles, and essays that often seem specifically designed to make your eyes glaze over—the reading comprehension passages being the worst offenders here. Another essay about poetry? Of all the things I don't give a damn about... it's sunny outside... I could be drinking a beer... et cetera, et cetera.

You have to nip that kind of daydreaming in the bud to ace this test. No matter how boring the content, your job is to figure that shit out. Slap yourself across the face if you need to. You must pay attention, you must understand whatever they're talking about, and you must find the right answer. This is why timing yourself is so important. The test takes place in 35-minute bursts, and you have to work steadily for the entire 35 minutes. You have to train yourself to focus in 35-minute increments, so your preparation might as well consist almost entirely of timed sections, followed by review.

How hard you can work.
The LSAT's Logic Games are a great example of this. The games are complex and confusing to most people when they first encounter them. But the games are also definitely something you can learn. (My students routinely see the biggest gains to their test scores on the Logic Games.)

There are hundreds of real LSAT Logic Games in circulation, and there's nothing stopping a diligent test prepper from doing all of them. I think this is quite intentional on the part of the LSAC. They want the test to be hard at first, but learnable with practice. Lawyers work their asses off. The LSAT wants to know if you're a lawyer. If you are, you'll work your ass off and improve dramatically at the test.

HOW TO STUDY FOR THE LSAT

One big difference between the LSAT and every other test you've ever taken is that all of the past tests are available to study. The December 2015 LSAT is available for sale as "PrepTest 77," and three more PrepTests get released every year. There is absolutely no substitute for doing these tests.

You don't have to do all of them, but you simply can't get the best score you're capable of unless you do at least 10 of them, and probably more like 20 or 30. Some of your crazy future lawyer competitors will do all of them. Some will do them more than once. I got a phone call from a student one day who was working her way through all 70-something tests for the third time. This time, she said, she was writing out a full explanation of each question as part of her review. I believe this student was on her second or third year of LSAT studying.

Now, that's clearly insane. I don't recommend you take that long, but I do recommend you study for at least a couple of months (the average is probably 3-4 months) and work through as many real, recent LSAT tests as you can.

You don't need to do all four sections of a practice test back-to-back-to-back-to-back. In fact, I'd probably prefer you don't. The name of the game is timed sections (35 minutes for most people, 1.5x or 2.5x that if you are granted accommodations by the LSAC for a disability), followed by thorough review of your mistakes. If you did just one of these sections per day, you'd be doing almost two tests per week. Do this for a few months, and you've got 20-something tests under your belt. This "slow drip" is probably the best way to learn. The LSAT is a test of logic, not a test of memory. You can't cram for it. Do a little bit every day, for a long period of time. Not only is this effective, but it's also a lot more civilized than trying to shoehorn 16 hours of studying into a weekend to make up for a week of slacking.

WHEN SHOULD I TAKE THE LSAT?

Most people should start studying for the LSAT as soon as possible. A slightly different but no less common question is "When should I take the test?" That's a much tougher question, and one only you can really answer. But here are the major factors to consider:

Through 2018, the LSAT will only be offered four times a year (February, June, September, and either mid-November or early December). Beginning in 2019, however, the LSAT will be offered more frequently, including dates in January, March, June, and July.

It takes three weeks to get your score back.

Law schools start accepting applications for next year in fall of THIS year. As soon as they start accepting applications, they start admitting students and giving away all their scholarship money. This is known as "rolling admissions." That means it's in your best interest to have your applications ready to go at the beginning of the admissions cycle. If you wait until later in the cycle, there will be fewer seats available, and little to no scholarship money. Most students don't want to hear this, but this means many of you will be better served by waiting an extra year before starting law school. It comes down to this: Would you rather start now and pay full price at whatever school will have you? Or would you rather wait a year and go to a better school, possibly for free? The choice is yours.

When preparing for the LSAT, everybody eventually reaches a plateau in terms of scores/understanding. When you're at that plateau, if you're not going to do something different with your preparation to break out to a new plateau (like a different teacher, different books, etc.) then it's probably time to take the LSAT.

Many schools only count your highest LSAT score, which means that taking the test more than once can be advantageous. You should schedule one real test date and at least one backup date, in case you don't have your best day the first time out. (If you score way worse than your practice test average, then you should definitely take it again.)

Bottom line: When you add all that up, most students who are just starting out should probably go ahead and register for a test that is two or three months from now. You may or may not be ready by then, but signing up will help motivate you to study. If you're not ready, you can always move your test date back—with a few weeks notice and a small LSAC fee, of course.

A Sample Timeline

Your LSAT score is a huge part of the admissions criteria for law school, so planning when you're going to take the test is definitely something that requires some fore-thought. There are no set rules as far as how early you should start prepping for the LSAT, but the ideal timeline would be approximately two years before your desired first day of law school.

Now, please note that this is a *perfect* timeline, and perfect rarely exists in the real world. Don't freak out if you're behind that schedule. The point I'm trying to make here is that many students do end up needing a full two years to prep for the LSAT, take the LSAT one or more times, and get their applications in early. If you're a freshman or sophomore in college, and want to go straight to law school after undergrad, you might be able to follow this timeline exactly. That's great. Otherwise, tweak these targets to fit your own schedule. The point is: start early.

			Summer/Fall	December
YEAR 0			Start studying for the LSAT	Take the LSAT (first attempt)

	February	June	September	
YEAR 1	Backup Test #1	Backup Test #2	Apply to Law School	

				Fall
YEAR 2				Begin Law School

4 LSAT Myths That Are 100% Bullshit

Most students arrive on the first night of class believing at least one of the following four statements. They're all dead wrong.

MYTH #1: YOU SHOULD ONLY TAKE THE LSAT ONCE

I still hear this from prelaw advisors from time to time, and it's a sure sign that your advisor should be advised to advise elsewhere. Yes, of course, we're going to do our damnedest to get our best LSAT score on the first try. But, there is no penalty for taking the test more than once and law schools really only care about our highest score, despite what you might have heard.

If we hit a home run on our first attempt, obviously we're celebrating. But if we swing and miss, or foul one off, we'd be fools not to swing a second time, and a third time if necessary. Hope for the best, but plan for the worst. You don't just need a test date, but a test date and at least one backup date. (Preferably two, just in case.) Having a backup plan can also help calm your nerves on your first attempt, by the way.

MYTH #2: YOU NEED TO FINISH EACH SECTION TO SCORE WELL

Every 35 minutes, the LSAT presents you with about 25 questions. That's roughly 85 seconds per question: plenty of time for anybody to answer, but not enough time for most mortals to also answer them correctly. News flash: You have to get them right to get a good score.

Here's the key: The questions at the beginning of each section are easier, often *vastly* easier, than the questions at the end. On the first night of class, I can easily spot the naive students rushing through the early questions, missing tons of the easy ones, in a doomed sprint toward the killer questions at the end. Often, they'll even finish early. But their accuracy, especially near the end of the section, will barely beat random guessing. Sadly, many of these students would miss the questions at the end even with unlimited time. If I could teach you only one thing about the LSAT, it would be this: Slow the fuck down.

Some quick illustrations of appropriate pacing:
- If you get 9 of the first 10 right and randomly guess on the remaining 15, getting three of those right, you'll score in the 140s. This should be your goal if you're currently in the 130s. If you can get 9 out of the first 10, you'll start to actually understand the test. Unsurprisingly, understanding leads to better speed and more accuracy.
- If you get 14 of first 15 right, and randomly guess on the remaining 10, getting two of those right, you'll score in the 150s. This should be your goal if you're currently in the 140s. Having achieved a new, higher understanding of the test, you will start to go faster, seemingly by accident.
- If you get 19 of first 20 right, and randomly guess on the remaining 5, getting one of those right, you'll score a 160-something. This should be your goal if you're currently in the 150s.
- When you reached the 160s, you've grasped the essentials and then you can start worrying about the LSAT's hardest questions. That means you're ready for the boss battle at the end of the level—questions 21-25. Until then, you can rest easy knowing that your current goal allows you to avoid these battles. You'll still get 1/5 of the hardest questions right just for filling in the bubbles.

MYTH #3: YOU SHOULD CLOSELY MONITOR THE TIME

The above guidelines are rough, and my intention is only to emphasize the importance of accuracy. I believe that you should always time yourself, but ignore the clock entirely. Focus purely on understanding the questions and getting them all right. Good scores come from long strings of correct answers. It doesn't matter how fast you're going if you don't get them right.

I always laugh when I see those special LSAT watches that some companies sell. They're allowable on the day of the test, because they're analog. They count down from 35 minutes at the click of a button, making them ideal for closely monitoring your time during each section. They're even color-coded in perfect 8 minute, 45 section chunks, so that you can "stay on pace" during the four logic games, or the four reading comprehension sections. Sadly, the answers are not printed on them. Every time you look at your watch—special LSAT timer nerd watch or otherwise—you are ignoring your primary duty, which is to answer the questions correctly.

Paying close attention to the time is, ironically, a major waste of it. I recommend that students not even bring a watch with them on the day of the test, to minimize the potential for distraction and panic. The proctor runs the official clock, and will give you a five-minute warning. If the proctor blows it somehow, which sometimes happens, don't worry: All the other LSAT nerds in the room will be frantically checking their special nerd watches, and they'll let the proctor know about the mistake. You should spend all 35 minutes calmly getting them right. There's negative value in watching the clock. All it can do is distract you and increase your panic.

MYTH #4: THE LOGIC GAMES ARE HARD

Everyone sucks at the Logic Games at first, but that's because they're different, and it absolutely does not mean that they are hard. If you're going to crash and burn on any section on your first attempt, this is probably it, because they're kinda weird and you're likely not used to stuff like this. Some students freeze up entirely, and refuse to even work for the entire 35 minutes on their first attempt; they just sit there looking shell-shocked. But once you get some reps in, the games turn out to be the easiest section of the test for many students. If you're going to reach a perfect score on any section, it's probably this one. Seriously.

Because the games are so learnable with practice (they're easily teachable in the classroom, with private tutoring, and especially by video), it's a huge opportunity for points. Don't give up! If you start with higher Reading Comprehension/Logical Reasoning scores, and lower Logic Games scores, you're an above-average candidate for improvement. Check out some of the free videos on my website (foxlsat.com) and you'll start to see what I mean. Through practice, you can absolutely conquer this most learnable section of the test.

Fox LSAT's

ONE
Thou Shalt Not Rush
(All Sections)

The biggest mistake most students make on the LSAT is trying to go way too damn fast. Each section has 22-27 questions, with a 35-minute time limit. You don't need to finish the sections in order to get a good score. As a matter of fact, most students (except those already scoring 165+) will hurt their score if they *do* try to finish. The earlier questions in each section are much easier than the later questions in each section. So if you try to rush, you are guaranteed to make silly mistakes on the earlier, easier questions. And the only upside is saving a few minutes to use on the later, harder questions—some of which are missable even with unlimited time. Go ahead and guess at the end of each section. (I recommend guessing all the same letter, so you can tell at a glance where your guesses began.) You'll still get one out of five right! Slow down, and invest your time making sure you get the earlier, easier questions right. A score of 160 is easily attainable without ever attempting the last five questions in each section. So if you're not already at 160, why the hell are you trying to finish the sections? *Speed comes from accuracy.* Not the other way around. If you slow down, and concentrate on getting them right, your mastery of the test will grow. And from mastery, you'll actually end up going faster. If you rush, you'll never improve.

Intentionally Blasphemous
Ten Commandments

TWO
Thou Shalt Be a Dick
(Logical Reasoning and Reading Comprehension)

The most important thing I can teach you about the verbal sections of the test (LR and RC) is that you should *argue* with the speaker. On the Logical Reasoning, at least half of the arguments are incomplete, if not outright bogus. As you read, try to call "bullshit" on the speaker. You can't do this too much with your friends and family, or they'll think you're a dick. But on the LSAT, you're allowed to let your dick flag fly. On the Logical Reasoning, always ask the speaker: *Oh yeah? What evidence do you have for that position?* This hyper-critical approach will allow you to see the holes in every argument. If you can see the holes, you can answer the questions. On the Reading Comprehension section, say to the author: *Why are you wasting my time with this?* This super-aggressive approach will allow you to cut through the bullshit and get to the author's main point.

THREE
Thou Shalt Combine the Rules Together
(Logic Games)

Most LSAT books talk about "making inferences," as if it's some sort of mystical secret that you can only learn on top of a mountain from a hairy dude who reeks of goat and patchouli. This shit is *not* magic! "Inferences" always come from combining the rules together. It's really that simple. Look at Rule 1, and see if you can combine it with Rule 2. Or Rule 3. Or Rule 4. If you don't see any connections there, then try to combine Rule 2 with Rule 3. Et cetera. Example:

> Rule 1: X comes before Y
> Rule 2: Y comes before Z

Mystical, magical inference combining Rule 1 and Rule 2: X must come before Z.

Did that hurt your head? I didn't think so. But most of your competition wouldn't take the time to see it! Most inferences are just like this: baby steps. Combine the rules together, and you'll be way ahead of the Logic Games.

FOUR
Thou Shalt Put a Gun to Thine Own Head
(Logic Games)

Slow down, damn it. On the Logic Games, you should be able to say, "The answer is B, and I would be willing to say this with a gun to my head," or with your house on the line, et cetera. The key to the Logic Games is understanding that there is a single, objectively correct answer to every question. There should be *zero* guessing involved. On the Logical Reasoning and Reading Comprehension, sometimes the answer will turn on a fine shade of meaning, and sometimes even an expert will be forced to say, "You know, I'm not 100% sure, but D just *feels* better than E." This *never* happens on the Logic Games. Answer every question with 100% certainty, even if this means devoting the entire 35 minutes to the first (of four) Logic Games and guessing on the remaining 16 or 17 questions. I'm serious. If you don't slow down and focus on getting them all right, you will never make any improvements.

If you do slow down, and get them all right on Game One, with 100 percent certainty, you will soon be on your way to getting them all right on Game Two. Students can make huge leaps on the Logic Games, but only if they focus on accuracy before speed. You should be *certain* that your chosen answer is correct. If not, you're doing it wrong.

FIVE
Thou Shalt Read the Goddamned Question
(All Sections)

Dominating the argument is imperative, but by itself that's not quite enough. You also have to—shocker!—answer the actual question you're being asked. On the Logical Reasoning section, sometimes they're asking you to be very evidence-based, like on Must Be True questions. But other times they allow you to fantasize, like on Sufficient Assumption questions. You have to know, and notice, the different question types. (Don't panic, there will be much more about Logical Reasoning later.)

This is also critical for the games. For example, they can ask "Which one of the following is a complete and accurate list..." or "Which one of the following *could be* a complete and accurate list..." Those two questions sound eerily similar, right? Yet they have entirely different answers; notice the subtle shift in the part I've italicized. On the LSAT, there won't be any italics. You'll need to go slowly, carefully, and read every word. Words matter! Especially when they're asking you the goddamned question.

SIX
Thou Shalt Remember that the Answer Choices are Not Thy Friend
(All Sections)

On Logical Reasoning and Reading Comprehension, if you're not occasionally eliminating all five answer choices, you're not being critical enough. (See Commandment Eight.) Remember that four out of five of the answer choices—eighty percent—are professionally written traps and time-wasters. Most students read the arguments way too quickly, and spend way too much time comparing the answer choices to each other—three or four, or even five of the answers might look good. This is exactly the wrong approach. A high scorer will always read the arguments and passages very carefully, make a prediction, and skim fairly quickly through the answer choices. Only one, or perhaps two, answers will even be remotely close to correct. But you can't easily eliminate the bad answers if you don't have an idea what you're looking for.

SEVEN
Thou Shalt Read All Five Answer Choices
(Logical Reasoning and Reading Comprehension)

Don't spend *forever* going through the answer choices, but definitely at least skim all five. Sometimes one of the earlier answer choices will be a very seductive trap, or almost indistinguishable from a later, better answer choice. If you don't read all five answer choices, you're going to get tricked. Go ahead and take the time to read B through E, even if you already love A. Most of the time, your first impulse will be correct. But once in a while, you'll realize that your first choice was actually second best. On the LSAT, there are no points for second best.

EIGHT
Thou Shalt Sometimes Eliminate All Five Answer Choices
(Logical Reasoning and Reading Comprehension)

If you don't occasionally dislike all five answer choices, you're not being critical enough. High scorers are super-critical of everything they read on the test, *especially* the answer choices. (Four out of five of them, after all, are wrong by definition.) Don't settle for an imperfect answer, unless you've already eliminated all five. When this does happen, you'll have to lower the bar a little bit, start back at the beginning, and choose the best of a bad lot.

NINE
Thou Shalt Know the Difference Between Sufficient and Necessary
(All Sections)

This is the first concept I teach to every class, and it's very simple. I need my head to live. My head is *necessary* to live. If I don't have my head, you know that I can *not* live. That's what "necessary" means.

If you see me come into the classroom and teach a four-hour LSAT class, then you know that I am alive—you have "sufficient information" to know that I must be alive. Seeing me teach a class is *sufficient, i.e.* enough, to know that I am alive. That's what "sufficient" means.

The LSAT will frequently confuse a necessary condition for a sufficient condition. Like this: "Nathan has his head, therefore we know he is alive." Uh, no. Nathan could very well be dead while still having a head. (As a matter of fact, he would strongly prefer to die that way.) Having a head is *necessary* for life, but it is not sufficient.

The LSAT will also frequently confuse a sufficient condition for a necessary condition. Like this: "Nathan wasn't in class tonight, therefore he must be dead." Uh, no. Nathan could be on the golf course somewhere, or he could be in a drunken stupor. Or, ideally, both! Being in LSAT class is *sufficient* for life, but it is not necessary.

I swear to God, that is all there is to the whole sufficient vs. necessary thing. It's easy, and it's the most commonly-tested flaw on the entire LSAT. Many students will pick up 5-10 LSAT points just by understanding this one simple concept. In the pages that follow, you'll find plenty of applications of this simple concept.

TEN
Thou Shalt Not Confuse Correlation with Causation

(Logical Reasoning)

This is the second concept that I teach to every class, and it's also very simple. I'll give you two examples of dumbass arguments that appear on every single LSAT. Ready? OK.

Dumbass argument one: Studies show that hangovers and lost credit cards are correlated. *Therefore, having a hangover causes you to lose your credit cards.*

The problem with this argument, I hope, is obvious. First, correlation doesn't prove causation. Second, specifically, how do we know that some other factor (the most obvious being drinking yourself silly) didn't cause *both* the hangover and the lost credit cards? If this "alternate cause" is true, it seems pretty ridiculous to say that hangovers are causing lost credit cards.

Dumbass argument two: Scientific studies have shown that people who eat poutine—that's French fries smothered in gravy and cheese curd, in case you've never been to Canada—tend to have more heart disease than people who do not eat poutine. *Therefore, heart disease causes people to eat poutine.*

The problem here is also, I hope, obvious. First, correlation doesn't prove causation. But specifically, how do we know that the poutine didn't cause the heart disease? Isn't that a more reasonable explanation?

Keep an eye out for these correlation-causation problems on the LSAT. You're sure to see examples in the pages to come.

Logical Reasoning

Logical Reasoning makes up two out of four scored sections on the LSAT—it's half the test. Each question is a short argument followed by a question and a set of five answer choices. Remember, most of the arguments presented on the LSAT will be bullshit. Your job is to *argue* with the speaker—Thou Shalt Be a Dick—and tell the speaker why his or her argument is bogus. If you can say why the argument is bullshit, you've almost won the battle. From there, all you need to do is pay attention to the *type* of question you're being asked (Strengthen, Weaken, et cetera) so you can pick the answer that does the job it needs to do.

On the following pages, you will find a discussion of each question type, with one or more sample question stems. Memorizing the examples for each type is helpful. But keep in mind that each type of question can be asked using a wide variety of specific language. For each question, you'll always need to read closely and think carefully about what they're asking. You'll get better with practice. It's simpler than you might think.

Flaw

Flaw questions tell you that there is a logical problem with the argument, and ask you to pick an answer choice that articulates the problem that exists.

Example Question Stems:
• Which one of the following most accurately describes a way in which the reasoning above is questionable?
• The argument is most vulnerable to criticism on the grounds that
• The reasoning in the argument is flawed because the argument
• Which one of the following most accurately describes a flaw in the reasoning above?

June **2007**
Section **2**
Question **21**

Driver: My friends say I will one day have an accident because I drive my sports car recklessly. But I have done some research, and apparently minivans and larger sedans have very low accident rates compared to sports cars. So trading my sports car in for a minivan would lower my risk of having an accident.

The reasoning in the driver's argument is most vulnerable to criticism on the grounds that this argument

A) infers a cause from a mere correlation
B) relies on a sample that is too narrow
C) misinterprets evidence that a result is likely as evidence that the result is certain
D) mistakes a condition sufficient for bringing about a result for a condition necessary for doing so
E) relies on a source that is probably not well-informed

The driver's argument makes me angry. Which is good—it means I'm paying attention.

Imagine you're this guy's friend—you're one of the friends that has been telling him he's going to die someday because he drives like an A-hole. He tells you, in response, that he's going to lower his risk of having an accident by switching to a minivan, which has a lower accident rate. What are you going to tell him?

My response would be something like this: "Minivans have lower accident rates because they're usually driven by Soccer Moms and other folks who drive safely. You, my soon-to-be-former friend, drive like an A-hole. Switching to a minivan is unlikely to stop you from driving like an A-hole. If you blast your new minivan around town like you're driving the A-Team van, I don't think the magical safety powers of the minivan are going to accrue to you. The way you drive, you'll likely make this thing dangerous."

Catch my drift? The driver has assumed that just because minivans are correlated with lower accident rates, that minivans must cause lower accident rates. That's a logical no-no. Correlation does not prove causation.

The question stem says "The reasoning in the driver's argument is most vulnerable to criticism on the grounds that this argument..." In other words, why is the argument bullshit? What's the flaw? I think the flaw is related to the correlation-causation problem I've already identified. Now it's time to go on to the answer choices.

A) Yep. This is exactly what I was looking for.

B) This is sometimes the correct answer, but it can only be the correct answer if the facts that were presented give us a solid reason to believe that the sample was too small or unrepresentative. We were given no such clues. No way.

C) This would be the answer if the argument had said "minivans have less accidents, so I definitely won't have any accidents in a minivan." That's not quite what the argument did, though.

D) This would be the answer if the argument had said "B.A. Baracus hates flying, so everyone who hates flying is B.A. Baracus." That's a common flaw on the LSAT, but it's not the flaw that actually happened here.

E) Just like B, this can only be the correct answer when we are given reason to believe that a source is biased. Here, the driver doesn't even mention any of his sources.

Our answer is A.

Weaken

Weaken Questions ask you to identify an answer choice that, *if true*, would poke a giant hole in the argument. Here's the subtle difference between a Flaw question and a Weaken question: On a Flaw question, you are asked to identify an *existing* problem with the argument. On a Weaken question you are asked to identify a *potential* problem with the argument.

Example Question Stems:
• Which of the following, if shown to be a realistic possibility, would undermine the argument?
• Which one of the following, as potential challenges, most seriously calls into question evidence offered in support of the conclusion above?
• Which one of the following, if true, most seriously weakens the support for the argument's conclusion?

> June **2007**
> Section **2**
> Question **5**

Scientist: Earth's average annual temperature has increased by about 0.5 degrees Celsius over the last century. This warming is primarily the result of the buildup of minor gases in the atmosphere, blocking the outward flow of heat from the planet.

Which one of the following, if true, would count as evidence against the scientist's explanation of Earth's warming?

A) Only some of the minor gases whose presence in the atmosphere allegedly resulted in the phenomenon described by the scientist were produced by industrial pollution.
B) Most of the warming occurred before 1940, while most of the buildup of minor gases in the atmosphere occurred after 1940.
C) Over the last century, Earth received slightly more solar radiation in certain years than it did in others.
D) Volcanic dust and other particles in the atmosphere reflect much of the Sun's radiation back into space before it can reach Earth's surface.
E) The accumulation of minor gases in the atmosphere has been greater over the last century than at any other time in Earth's history.

This one feels a little different, huh? That's because the argument, for once, seems close to being reasonable—there's no glaring flaw. All we have here is a description of a phenomenon and then an explanation of that phenomenon. There aren't a lot of moving parts. Still, the argument is far from complete.

According to the scientist, it's a fact that the Earth's average annual temperature has increased by about 0.5 degrees Celsius over the last century. We can't argue with this part. But the scientist goes on to explain this fact with a claim about causality: The warming is primarily the result of the buildup of gases in the atmosphere, which blocks the outward flow of heat from the planet.

Uh-oh. That's a claim of causation.

The LSAT has a field day with Cause and Effect arguments—I've seen Logical Reasoning sections where almost one half of the questions had something to do with Cause and Effect. Here, we are asked to identify "evidence against" the Scientist's explanation. Before I look at the answer choices, I'm going to think about two main problems that commonly pop up with this type of reasoning:

1) Is it possible that the Effect actually caused the alleged Cause? An obvious example of this is "Rich people own Bentleys, so Bentley ownership causes one to be rich." Silly, right? That's obviously backward. Well, we need to see if that might be happening in the Scientist's argument. Here, the Effect was global warming, and the purported cause was a buildup of greenhouse gases. So ask yourself: Is it possible that the Scientist has it the wrong way around? What if the warming actually caused the buildup of the gases? If that were true, then wouldn't the Scientist look silly for claiming that the gases caused the warming?

2) Is it possible that some other Cause actually caused both the purported Cause and Effect? An obvious example of this is "Smokers make a lot of new friends outside bars, and they also get a lot of cancer. So making a lot of new friends outside bars causes you to get cancer." Silly, right? Clearly smoking is the underlying cause both of making friends outside bars AND getting cancer. There's no causal relationship between making friends and getting cancer. So ask yourself: Is it possible that the Scientist is ignoring some other factor? We can get creative here. What if, I don't know, radiation from Uranus was causing both the temperature increase and the buildup of atmospheric gases? If that were true, then wouldn't the Scientist look silly for claiming that the gases caused the warming? (I'm sure that "Uranus" is not going to appear in the correct answer. But something that introduces a new factor like this could be perfect.)

I don't think either of these predictions is guaranteed to be correct. But both of these types of answers appear over and over and over as correct answers on old LSATs, so we have to look out for them. Okay, here we go. Remember, we're looking for the answer choice that would make the Scientist's argument look stupid:

A) This doesn't matter. The cause of the gases themselves really isn't in question here. They could have been caused by industrial pollution, automobiles, cattle, who cares? If Answer A were true, the Scientist would say "So what? The gases still caused global warming." We're looking for an answer choice that leaves the Scientist no reasonable response... we want to shut him up for good.

B) Hmm. If this is true, then the Scientist's purported Cause happened after the Scientist's purported Effect. Hey Scientist, I have a question for you: How can the gases have caused global warming if the global warming happened first? I like this answer, because the Scientist really can't say anything in response. (Also, notice that it kinda fits with my first prediction, the possibility that the warming actually caused the gases, instead of the other way around.) This one is a keeper.

C) Huh? Who cares. If this were true, the Scientist would say something like "My argument had nothing to do with solar radiation, but I'm not surprised that solar radiation fluctuates slightly from year to year. This does nothing to change the relationship between a buildup of atmospheric gases and the resulting global warming." There's no way this can be the answer.

D) Again, I don't see how this is relevant. The Scientist would say "I'm not surprised that volcanic dust reflects the Sun's radiation. This fact does nothing to change the relationship between a buildup of atmospheric gases and the resulting global warming."

E) This would actually strengthen the Scientist's argument, but we were looking for a weakener. If this were true, the Scientist would say "yes, yes... since the Earth has been warming over the past century, this fact confirms my hypothesis that a buildup of gases has been causing global warming."

The answer that most weakens the Scientist's argument is **B, so that's our answer**.

Strengthen

Strengthen questions present an argument, and then ask you to choose an answer that would most support the given argument. The correct answer on a Strengthen question will often be the opposite of something that would have weakened the argument.

Example Question Stems:
• Which of the following, if assumed, most helps to justify the reasoning above?
• Which one of the following, if true, most strengthens the argument?

> June **2007**
> Section **3**
> Question **13**

Therapist: Cognitive psychotherapy focuses on changing a patient's conscious beliefs. Thus, cognitive psychotherapy is likely to be more effective at helping patients overcome psychological problems than are forms of psychotherapy that focus on changing unconscious beliefs and desires, since only conscious beliefs are under the patient's direct conscious control.

Which one of the following, if true, would most strengthen the therapist's argument?

A) Psychological problems are frequently caused by unconscious beliefs that could be changed with the aid of psychotherapy.

B) It is difficult for any form of psychotherapy to be effective without focusing on mental states that are under the patient's direct conscious control.

C) Cognitive psychotherapy is the only form of psychotherapy that focuses primarily on changing the patient's conscious beliefs.

D) No form of psychotherapy that focuses on changing the patient's unconscious beliefs and desires can be effective unless it also helps change beliefs that are under the patient's direct conscious control.

E) All of a patient's conscious beliefs are under the patient's conscious control, but other psychological states cannot be controlled effectively without the aid of psychotherapy.

34   INTRODUCING THE LSAT

LSAT arguments frequently don't make sense, but sometimes they can be forced to make a little more sense by rearranging them slightly. This question is a good example of this strategy.

With the exact same facts, and exact same conclusion, the argument is a lot easier to follow if it's rearranged like this:

> Therapist: Only conscious beliefs are under the patient's direct conscious control. Cognitive psychotherapy focuses on changing a patient's conscious beliefs. Thus, cognitive psychotherapy is likely to be more effective at helping patients overcome psychological problems than are forms of psychotherapy that focus on changing unconscious beliefs and desires.

To me, that makes a lot more sense... it's easier to follow an argument when it starts with the evidence, and finishes with the conclusion. The conclusion of this argument is "cognitive psychotherapy is likely to be more effective at helping patients overcome psychological problems than are forms of psychotherapy that focus on changing unconscious beliefs and desires." Why does the therapist believe this? Well, "only conscious beliefs are under a patient's direct conscious control, and cognitive psychotherapy focuses on changing a patient's conscious beliefs."

The argument, rearranged, is now easier to follow. But that doesn't mean it's a good argument. There's a hole here, isn't there? I think so, because it assumes that "conscious control" is required, or at least helpful, for patients to overcome psychological problems. Imagine if I were arguing with the therapist, and I said something like this:

> Nathan: Bullshit! Many psychological problems have nothing to do with conscious beliefs, or things that are under the patient's direct conscious control. Therefore hypnotism, and other forms of psychotherapy that focus on the unconscious, are every bit as effective as cognitive psychotherapy, and in many cases even more effective than cognitive psychotherapy.

I think that's a pretty strong attack, and you should always be trying to launch your own against the speaker after reading their argument. Remember Commandment Two: Thou Shalt Be a Dick!

Having said that, I now feel equipped to see what the question is asking: Which one of the following, if true, would most strengthen the therapist's argument?

Since we've already come up with a strong attack against the argument, we know what its weakness is—and how we can strengthen the argument by defending it against that attack. Our attack basically boils down to "conscious beliefs and conscious control are unimportant when it comes to overcoming psychological problems." So a great defense against that attack would be "conscious beliefs and conscious control are necessary in order for a patient to overcome psychological problems. (Stated in a somewhat different way, "conscious beliefs and control are the only way for a patient to overcome psychological problems.")

Let's see if we can find something like that in the answer choices:

A) This would weaken the argument, and we were asked to strengthen it. So this is out.

B) I love this answer. It is very similar to "conscious control is necessary." It's a great fit with our prediction.

C) Nope... not as good as B. This answer, if true, does nothing to show that conscious beliefs are important when trying to fix psychological problems. So this answer doesn't protect the argument's major weakness.

D) This is a bizarre answer, because it mixes the two different types of psychotherapy (conscious and unconscious) that were being compared in the argument. This is just a mess. What do hybrid forms of therapy have to do with the therapist's argument?

E) This answer is another mess... it takes a bunch of concepts from the therapist's argument, puts them in a blender, and pours out a bucket of mystery slop. I don't see how this statement, if true, would eliminate unconscious forms of psychotherapy.

Our answer is B.

The best way to get past D and E on this question is to positively identify B as something that would strengthen the argument by defending it. As I've said, you must predict the answers in advance. If you find yourself spending a lot of time in the answer choices, comparing one against the other, you are doing it wrong. You must engage with the arguments deeply enough to be able to understand what's missing before you even get to the answer choices. If you can do that, then only one (or sometimes perhaps two) answers will look attractive at all—the others can be easily skipped. This is a much faster and much more accurate way to attack the LSAT.

Sufficient Assumption

Sufficient Assumption questions give you an incomplete argument, and then ask you to pick an answer choice that would, if true, make the argument complete. Whereas a Strengthen question only requires an answer that would make the argument stronger, a Sufficient Assumption question requires an answer that would make the argument's conclusion unavoidable. In other words, a Sufficient Assumption question is looking for the answer that would make the argument win.

Example Question Stems:
- Which one of the following, if assumed, would allow the conclusion above to be properly drawn?
- The conclusion drawn follows logically from the premises if which of the following is assumed?
- The conclusion is properly inferred if which one of the following is assumed?

June **2007**
Section **2**
Question **6**

An undergraduate degree is necessary for appointment to the executive board. Further, no one with a felony conviction can be appointed to the board. Thus, Murray, an accountant with both a bachelor's and a master's degree, cannot be accepted for the position of Executive Administrator, since he has a felony conviction.

The argument's conclusion follows logically if which one of the following is assumed?

A) Anyone with a master's degree and without a felony conviction is eligible for appointment to the executive board.
B) Only candidates eligible for appointment to the executive board can be accepted for the position of Executive Administrator.
C) An undergraduate degree is not necessary for acceptance for the position of Executive Administrator.
D) If Murray did not have a felony conviction, he would be accepted for the position of Executive Administrator.
E) The felony charge on which Murray was convicted is relevant to the duties of the position of Executive Administrator.

The answer to this question, as usual, is to be found in the argument itself. Read carefully. Read slowly. Read it twice if you have to. Go ahead, I'll be here when you come back.

You could probably diagram this question, but the problem with diagramming is that you add a level of abstraction to your thinking, making it easy to misunderstand the argument and introduce silly mistakes. I end up doing a diagram for maybe one or two questions per test. (Basically, only when I'm in trouble and can't think of any other way to do it.) This isn't one of those times, because I already know why the argument is bullshit. The argument is bullshit because it has assumed (rather than stated) that the position of Executive Administrator is on the executive board.

When I say "assumed," what I mean is that the argument has left out a key piece of evidence. Here, the argument never specifically says that the position of Executive Administrator is an executive board position. Sure, it sounds like it's a board position. But that's not enough. The speaker here needs to specifically state that fact. If it's true, then I think the logic is pretty tight. There's a premise (i.e., stated evidence) that says nobody with a felony conviction can serve on the board. There's a premise that says Murray has a felony conviction. If it's also true that the Executive Administrator is on the executive board, then I would be forced to conclude that Murray can't be on the board.

I haven't even looked at the question yet, let alone the answer choices. But since I now know what the argument is missing, I'm already 90% of the way to answering whatever the question may be.

The question here says "The argument's conclusion follows logically if which one of the following is assumed?" This is what's known as a Sufficient Assumption question. What it really means is "which one of the following would prove the conclusion of the argument?" ("Follows logically" simply means "is proven" on the LSAT.)

I love Sufficient Assumption questions, because the answers are really easy to predict. To prove the argument's conclusion, the correct answer simply must cover up the hole in the argument that I have discussed above. The correct answer must somehow connect the position of Executive Administrator to the executive board. Here are a few predictions for what the correct answer might be:

1) "The Executive Administrator is on the executive board." (clean and simple.)
2) "Any job Murray would apply for would be on the executive board." (kind of a weird backdoor, but it would work.)
3) "All jobs in the world are on the executive board." (overkill, but definitely sufficient.)

I think the correct answer is probably going to be something very similar to #1. But I'm not afraid of answers like #2 or #3 here, even though they might seem too strong. Some questions on the LSAT prefer strongly-stated answers. Sufficient Assumption questions fall into this category. It's okay if the correct answer goes overboard here, as long as it proves that Murray can't get the job. Let's look at the answer choices:

A) We were asked to prove that Murray is not eligible for the board. This answer choice couldn't be used to prove that Murray actually is eligible for the board, but that's not the same thing as proving he's not eligible. Furthermore this answer doesn't connect the Executive Administrator position to the board, which is an important connection here. Let's keep looking.

B) Okay, this one would do it. It's not exactly what I predicted, but if this is true then Murray isn't eligible for the job, and that's what we need to prove. We know he is ineligible for the board because of the felony conviction. If the Executive Administrator position has the same requirements as the board, then Murray is out of luck. Mission accomplished. I am 99.9% certain this will be the correct answer. Still, I'll always quickly read the rest of the answer choices just in case.

C) This answer, if true, makes it easier to get the job, not harder. We want to prove that Murray *can't* get the job. (Furthermore, it's irrelevant to Murray because he does have a bachelor's degree.) This answer is bad. Very bad.

D) Sure, and if your grandma had balls, she'd be your grandpa. Murray does have a felony conviction, so this answer is useless. We're trying to prove that Murray can't get the job, and this answer choice could only be used to prove that he *could* get the job (if he didn't have the conviction, which he does.) This is a comedically bad answer, just like C.

E) No. The "duties" of the position are irrelevant. I suppose this answer choice strengthens the case that Murray shouldn't get the job. (If Murray was convicted of embezzlement, and this is an accounting position, then that would seem to be a strike against him.) But answer B *proves* that Murray can't get the job. We need to prove our case here, not just strengthen it.

So our answer is B.

Necessary Assumption

Necessary Assumption questions present an incomplete argument, and then ask you to identify the critical missing piece. The correct answer, if untrue, will ruin the argument. In other words, a Necessary Assumption question is asking for the answer that must be true, or else the argument will lose.

Example Question Stems:
• Which one of the following is an assumption on which the argument depends?
• The argument makes which one of the following assumptions
• Which one of the following is an assumption required by the argument?

June **2007**
Section **3**
Question **17**

When exercising the muscles in one's back, it is important, in order to maintain a healthy back, to exercise the muscles on opposite sides of the spine equally. After all, balanced muscle development is needed to maintain a healthy back, since the muscles on opposite sides of the spine must pull equally in opposing directions to keep the back in proper alignment and protect the spine.

Which one of the following is an assumption required by the argument?

A) Muscles on opposite sides of the spine that are equally well developed will be enough to keep the back in proper alignment.
B) Exercising the muscles on opposite sides of the spine unequally tends to lead to unbalanced muscle development.
C) Provided that one exercises the muscles on opposite sides of the spine equally, one will have a generally healthy back.
D) If the muscles on opposite sides of the spine are exercised unequally, one's back will be irreparably damaged.
E) One should exercise daily to ensure that the muscles on opposite sides of the spine keep the back in proper alignment.

This question is easy if you argue, and impossible if you don't. You have to argue a lot on the LSAT, and you have to argue every last detail there is to argue. Let me show you what I mean:

> When exercising the muscles in one's back, it is important, in order to maintain a healthy back, to exercise the muscles on opposite sides of the spine equally.

Oh reeeeeeeeeallllllly?!?! You might be right about that, but you also might be completely full of shit. Maybe I like working out just one side of my back, and maybe my back is in perfect shape. What's the evidence for your assertion that I need to exercise both sides equally? Huh buddy? Let's hear it.

> After all, balanced muscle development is needed to maintain a healthy back, since the muscles on opposite sides of the spine must pull equally in opposing directions to keep the back in proper alignment and protect the spine.

Yeah, well, I still don't believe you. What does "balanced muscle development" have to do with exercise? I mean, sure, it might be reasonable to think that working out affects muscle development. But "reasonable" doesn't cut it on the LSAT. I didn't see any evidence on that. Where's your proof that exercise affects muscle development? Your argument is incomplete until you can prove that point.

The question asks: "Which one of the following is an assumption required by the argument?" Through arguing, we've already answered this Necessary Assumption question. The argument has left something out: "Exercise affects muscle development." That's necessary because if exercise does *not* affect muscle development, then the argument can't possibly make any sense. All of the holes in the argument's logic must be filled to satisfy this question. And now we know exactly what we're looking for, before even looking at the answer choices. Piece of cake.

A) We have a really strong prediction here, and this doesn't match that prediction. We don't even need to give it a second thought, unless we look at all five answers and don't find what we're looking for.
B) Bingo. This answer bridges the critical gap between "exercise" and "muscle development." If this answer is untrue, it would ruin the logic of the argument. That means it's a Necessary Assumption of the argument, and is going to be our answer.
C) No way. The argument never said anything about "general health." This answer can't possibly be something that's required by the argument. Plus we've already found a perfect answer, in B.
D) This is wrong for the same reason as C. The argument never said anything about "irreparable damage." This answer can't possibly be something that's required by the argument.
E) Same thing as C and D. The argument said nothing about "daily exercise."

Our answer is B, because it must be true or else the argument will fail. That's the definition of "Necessary." We're not always able to predict the answers so easily, but it's awful nice when it happens. Remember to slow down, in order to allow yourself to make the connections more frequently. You'll pick up time in the long run.

Must Be True

Must Be True questions give you a series of facts, and then ask you to identify an answer choice that must also be true, if the given facts are true.

Example Question Stems:
• Which one of the following must be true if the statements above are correct?
• The above statements, if true, most strongly support which one of the following?
• Which of the following is most strongly supported by the information above?

June **2007**
Section **2**
Question **18**

Modern science is built on the process of posing hypotheses and testing them against observations—in essence, attempting to show that the hypotheses are incorrect. Nothing brings more recognition than overthrowing conventional wisdom. It is accordingly unsurprising that some scientists are skeptical of the widely accepted predictions of global warming. What is instead remarkable is that with hundreds of researchers striving to make breakthroughs in climatology, very few find evidence that global warming is unlikely.

The information above provides the most support for which one of the following statements?

A) Most scientists who are reluctant to accept the global warming hypothesis are not acting in accordance with the accepted standards of scientific debate.
B) Most researchers in climatology have substantial motive to find evidence that would discredit the global warming hypothesis.
C) There is evidence that conclusively shows that the global warming hypothesis is true.
D) Scientists who are skeptical about global warming have not offered any alternative hypotheses to explain climatological data.
E) Research in global warming is primarily driven by a desire for recognition in the scientific community.

For once, a well-reasoned argument.

It concludes, "it is remarkable that very few researchers find evidence that global warming is unlikely." Why is this remarkable? Well, global warming is "widely accepted," and there are hundreds of researchers striving to break through, and nothing attracts recognition more than overthrowing conventional wisdom. *Therefore*, it's remarkable that the researchers aren't finding anything. This actually makes sense.

The question stem says: "The information above provides the most support for which one of the following statements."

The LSAC, in its typically clunky way, calls this type of question "Identifying a Position that is Conclusively Proven by the Information Provided." That's too much of a mouthful for me, so let's just call this question type "Must Be True." They're extremely common.

This question type can be tricky when you first start studying for the LSAT, because you might be inclined to pass up answer choices that seem "too obvious." Don't do that! Be open to the possibility that you're actually plenty smart enough to punch this test in the face. On a question of this type, all you're looking for is the one answer that has been proven by the speaker's statements (and nothing more than the speaker's statements—outside information is not allowed). The correct answer does not have to be the speaker's main point, nor does the speaker's entire statement have to be related to the correct answer. If any part of the speaker's statement proves that an answer choice has to be true, then that's your answer. This question type is pretty easy once you get the hang of it.

I can't predict the answer here, because there's no glaring flaw in the logic. Rather, I just have to check out each answer choice and pick the one that, as conservatively as possible, has been proven by the information provided. What I mean by "conservative" is that I'm going to avoid any answer choice that is even slightly speculative. The correct answer is not something that is probably true, or something that I know to be true in real life—it's something that is true according to the facts on the page.

A) I don't think we were told anything about the behavior of any of the scientists (let alone most of them) who question global warming. (All we know is they exist, and they haven't found much yet. We have no idea if they're behaving or misbehaving.) This answer is not supported by the given facts, so it's out.

B) The "motive" that we were given is that 1) global warming is widely accepted and 2) overturning the conventional wisdom leads to recognition. I'm not 100% sure that "most researchers in climatology" have this motive, however. I'd like this answer more if it said "some" instead of "most," because that's a much lower standard to prove. Still, we can pick B if the rest of the answers suck.

C) What? No. We know nothing about the evidence for global warming. All we know is that there isn't much compelling evidence against it.

D) Uh, I don't think so. We were told that "very few researchers" have found evidence against global warming. That doesn't mean there is zero evidence, and it certainly doesn't mean that there aren't any competing theories out there.

E) We're told that recognition is one motive, but we're not told that it's the primary motive. Other motives could be money, or altruism, or plain old nerdy love of learning. The word "primary" disqualifies this answer choice instantly.

I didn't love B, but it's the least speculative of the answer choices. **So our answer is B.**

Main Conclusion

Main Conclusion questions present an argument, and simply ask you to identify the argument's main point. Ask the speaker, "Why are you wasting my time with this?" to help you zero in on the main idea.

Example Question Stems:
• Which one of the following most accurately expresses the arguments conclusion?
• Of the following, which one most accurately expresses the conclusion drawn above?

June **2007**
Section **3**
Question **12**

Novel X and Novel Y are both semiautobiographical novels and contain many very similar themes and situations, which might lead one to suspect plagiarism on the part of one of the authors. However, it is more likely that the similarity of themes and situations in the two novels is merely coincidental, since both authors are from very similar backgrounds and have led similar lives.

Which one of the following most accurately expresses the conclusion drawn in the argument?

A) Novel X and Novel Y are both semiautobiographical novels, and the two novels contain many very similar themes and situations.

B) The fact that Novel X and Novel Y are both semiautobiographical novels and contain many very similar themes and situations might lead one to suspect plagiarism on the part of one of the authors.

C) The author of Novel X and the author of Novel Y are from very similar backgrounds and have led very similar lives.

D) It is less likely that one of the authors of Novel X or Novel Y is guilty of plagiarism than that the similarity of themes and situations in the two novels is merely coincidental.

E) If the authors of Novel X and Novel Y are from very similar backgrounds and have led similar lives, suspicions that either of the authors plagiarized are very likely to be unwarranted.

When trying to find the main conclusion of an argument, the order in which the elements are presented is irrelevant. The conclusion can be first, last, or somewhere in the middle. Keywords can provide clues. When the argument says "so," or "therefore," they're probably giving the conclusion of the argument. And when they say "because," "since," or "for," they're probably giving evidence. But what if they don't feed you the keywords? You can still figure out the conclusion by thinking about which parts support the others. Here's a simple example:

"We should order a pizza. I'm hungry."

What's the conclusion there? Does the first sentence support the second? Or does the second sentence support the first? Try it both ways: "We should order a pizza, THEREFORE I'm hungry." Does that make sense? No, not really. Let's try it the other way: "I'm hungry, THEREFORE we should order a pizza." Sounds much better, right? So "We should order a pizza" is the conclusion of the argument.

Now, try this same technique with the main elements of the argument on the previous page: "The similarity of themes and situations in the two novels is probably coincidental, THEREFORE the authors are from similar backgrounds and have led similar lives?" No way, that just doesn't sound right. Try it the other way: "The authors are from similar backgrounds and have led similar lives, THEREFORE the similarity of themes and situations in the two novels is probably coincidental." Sounds much better. So "The similarity of themes and situations in the two novels is probably coincidental" is the conclusion of the argument.

A) This doesn't match our prediction. We need "coincidental," or a synonym, in our answer.

B) This was the first sentence of the argument, but the speaker went on to say "actually, it's probably just coincidental." So this can't be the author's main point.

C) This was evidence that supports the author's main point, but not the main point itself.

D) This is the best answer so far. It comes closest to matching our prediction.

E) This goes further than the speaker actually went. The speaker says "it's probably not plagiarism," but that doesn't mean that the author thinks suspicion of plagiarism is unwarranted. Furthermore, the facts already state that the two authors are from very similar backgrounds, so this answer is nonsensical when it starts off with "If they are from similar backgrounds, then..." We already know they are from similar backgrounds!

Our answer is D, because it best matches the author's main conclusion. This is a very basic type of question. Master this one first, before proceeding to other, more difficult, types of questions.

Agree/Disagree

Agree/Disagree questions present a conversation between two speakers, and ask you to choose an answer on which the two speakers agree or disagree. Listen carefully to the two speakers: Do they agree on their evidence? Do they agree on the conclusion that can be drawn from the evidence?

Example Question Stems:
- "Robert" and "Sarah" have committed to disagreeing on which of the following?
- "Beth's" and "Carmen's" statements provide the most support for the claim that they would disagree about whether
- The dialogue most strongly supports the claim that "Chris" and "Joe" disagree about which one of the following?
- Their dialogue provides the most support for the claim that "Antonio" and "Ben" agree that

June **2007**
Section **3**
Question **7**

Antonio: One can live a life of moderation by never deviating from the middle course. But then one loses the joy of spontaneity and misses the opportunities that come to those who are occasionally willing to take great chances, or to go too far.

Marla: But one who, in the interests of moderation, never risks going too far is actually failing to live a life of moderation: one must be moderate even in one's moderation.

Antonio and Marla disagree over

A) whether it is desirable for people occasionally to take great chances in life
B) what a life of moderation requires of a person
C) whether it is possible for a person to embrace other virtues along with moderation
D) how often a person ought to deviate from the middle course in life
E) whether it is desirable for people to be moderately spontaneous

This question presents a conversation between two people, Antonio and Marla. The question asks what "Antonio and Marla disagree over," so the task here is to figure out what Antonio and Marla are really fighting about. Are they fighting about the evidence? If so, which part of the evidence? Or do they agree about the evidence, but disagree about what that evidence means, i.e., the conclusion? Let's see.

You can usually predict this sort of question in advance with a reasonable degree of certainty, since the question only makes sense if the two speakers' statements prove that they disagree about something. Here goes: Antonio says moderation causes one to "lose the joy of spontaneity" and "miss the opportunities that come to those who... take great chances or go too far." Marla says that the kind of moderation that causes one to never risk going too far is actually a failure to live moderately; she concludes that "one must be moderate even in one's moderation."

This conversation greatly bores me, but I still think we can answer the question. Basically, they are arguing about the nature of moderation. Antonio says one can be moderate by never taking risks, Marla says one must take some risks to be moderate.

Let's make this more interesting by pretending they're talking about beer. Antonio thinks one can be "moderate" by never drinking any beer at all, Marla thinks one can NOT be "moderate" with this kind of teetotaling. Marla would advise that to be "moderate" a person should have a beer now and again (but don't go too far and end up in the gutter).

Make sense? Let's see if we've predicted the answer:

A) Nope. All they're arguing about is the definition of "moderation." Neither speaker has taken a position on whether or not moderation, or taking chances, is desirable.

B) I think this is probably it. This basically means "they are arguing about the definition of moderation."

C) Definitely not. Neither speaker talks about the compatibility of "other virtues" (honesty, perhaps) with moderation.

D) Nope. Same explanation as A.

E) Nope, same explanation as A and D.

So our answer is B. Predict the answer to this type of question in advance! Don't look at the answer choices until you've got a very good idea what the real argument is about.

Explanation

Explanation questions present an apparent mystery, and ask you to choose an answer choice that would explain this mystery. It's critical to understand what the mystery is before looking at the answer choices: If you don't know what crime you're trying to solve, how can you evaluate suspects?

Example Question Stems:
• Which one of the following, if true, contributes most to an explanation of the puzzling situation described above?
• Which of the following, if true, most helps to resolve the apparent discrepancy above?
• Which one of the following, if true, contributes to a resolution of the apparent paradox?

> June **2007**
> Section **2**
> Question **25**

During the nineteenth century, the French academy of art was a major financial sponsor of painting and sculpture in France; sponsorship by private individuals had decreased dramatically by this time. Because the academy discouraged innovation in the arts, there was little innovation in nineteenth century French sculpture. Yet nineteenth century French painting showed a remarkable degree of innovation.

Which one of the following, if true, most helps to explain the difference between the amount of innovation in French painting and the amount of innovation in French sculpture during the nineteenth century?

A) In France in the nineteenth century, the French academy gave more of its financial support to painting than it did to sculpture.

B) The French academy in the nineteenth century financially supported a greater number of sculptors than painters, but individual painters received more support, on average, than individual sculptors.

C) Because stone was so much more expensive than paint and canvas, far more unsponsored paintings were produced than were unsponsored sculptures in France during the nineteenth century.

D) Very few of the artists in France in the nineteenth century who produced sculptures also produced paintings.

E) Although the academy was the primary sponsor of sculpture and painting, the total amount of financial support that French sculptors and painters received from sponsors declined during the nineteenth century.

In this question, we're told that the French academy of art was "a major financial sponsor" of both painting and sculpture in France in the 19th century. We're also told that the academy "discouraged innovation in the arts." But then we're told a puzzling fact: French sculpture during that period showed little innovation, while French painting showed a lot of innovation. Why would this be?

The question says exactly that: "Which one of the following, if true, most helps to explain the difference between the amount of innovation in French painting and the amount of innovation in French sculpture during the nineteenth century?"

You've gotta let your natural curiosity get aroused here: If the academy was funding both painters and sculptors, and "discouraged innovation," then why would the painters go on innovating while the sculptors didn't? The correct answer must EXPLAIN this mystery.

Before looking at the answer choices, I have a few ideas:

1) Maybe the painters were more often funded by a lot of other sources, for example wealthy patrons, so maybe the painters weren't as beholden to the anti-innovation academy. Maybe the sculptors had no other funding. If this scenario is true, it would be a good explanation for why the painters kept innovating but the sculptors didn't.
2) Maybe painters are just naturally ballsier than sculptors. Maybe the painters didn't care if the academy kicked them out on the street. Maybe the painters were all single bohemians, while the sculptors had families to support. If this scenario is true, it explains the innovation discrepancy.
3) Maybe there was simply no room to innovate in sculpture at the time–maybe everything had already been invented in sculpture. Maybe painting, on the other hand, was ripe for innovation at the time. This scenario is unlikely, perhaps... but if it's true, it explains the innovation discrepancy.

One last thing before looking at the answers. Let me tell you an answer that would certainly NOT be correct: "Contrary to previous accounts, there was actually quite a lot of innovation in French sculpture in the 19th century." There is no way in hell that would be the correct answer, because it doesn't "explain" anything. Instead, that would just say, "Oh, actually, there was no mystery in the first place." This type of answer is like a mystery/suspense movie where the lead character wakes up at the end of the movie and oooooooooooh... IT WAS ALL A DREAM! That's not an explanation! That's cheating! The correct answer on an LSAT "Explanation" question must actually EXPLAIN something.

Okay, our curiosity has been aroused. We really want to know why there was innovation in painting but not in sculpture. (If we're not actually interested, we're going to fake interest in hopes of actually getting interested.) So let's find the answer choice that makes us go "OHHHHHH, I see! That makes sense."

A) This, if true, would actually make it harder to understand why the painters kept innovating and the sculptors didn't. No way.

B) I don't think so. If each individual painter was getting *more* money from the academy than each individual sculptor, wouldn't that make the painters more likely to bow to the wishes of the academy? This answer, like A, actually seems to muddy the waters instead of making things clear.

C) Ahh, now this makes sense. This answer, if true, provides a good reason why sculptors had to do what the academy wanted (stone was too expensive to buy without academy support) but painters could continue innovating (because they could still sneak out and buy some canvas and produce whatever they wanted). This seems like an explanation, so it might be the answer. It's certainly better than A and B.

D) So what? This says "the sculptors and painters were mostly two different groups of people," but it doesn't even start to explain why one group continued innovating while the other group did not. No way.

E) Again, this answer makes no distinction between the circumstances and motivations of painters and those of sculptors. How can this explain anything about the difference in behavior of the two groups?

Luckily, C was a good explanation... **so our answer is C**.

Complete the Argument

Complete the Argument questions present you with an incomplete argument, and then ask you to choose an answer that represents what should come next. Don't speculate! It's not about where the argument might go; it's about where the argument is already going.

Example Question Stems:
• Which one of the following most logically completes the argument?
• The conclusion of the argument above is most strongly supported if which one of the following completes the argument?
• Which one of the following most reasonably completes the argument?

June **2007**
Section **2**
Question **3**

A century in certain ways is like a life, and as the end of a century approaches, people behave toward that century much as someone who is nearing the end of life does toward that life. So just as people in their last years spend much time looking back on the events of their life, people at a century's end _____.

Which one of the following most logically completes the argument?

A) reminisce about their own lives
B) fear that their own lives are about to end
C) focus on what the next century will bring
D) become very interested in the history of the century just ending
E) reflect on how certain unfortunate events of the century could have been avoided

This question is a relatively rare type of question—maybe it appears once per test. Rather than containing a flawed or weak argument, it simply gives you the beginning of an argument and asks you to fill in the blank. So rather than saying "this argument is bullshit because _____," like we usually do, we're going to complete the argument in a way that is not bullshit. So what do I mean by that?

Well, basically, we just want to complete the argument in a way that logically connects with the evidence provided. We're going to be conservative here. We don't want to go further than what the evidence warrants, and we're going to avoid huge assumptions, and wild, outlandish or speculative statements that aren't justified by the evidence.

If the evidence had said "A=B, and B=C, therefore _____." it would be totally reasonable to say "A=C," because that's been proven by the facts and it kinda seems like that's where the argument was headed. But we certainly wouldn't come with "A=D," or "Everything equals C" or "X equals Y," because then you'd be bringing in outside information and speculation and making shit up. No great leaps of intuition are required here. You don't need to be Sherlock Holmes. All you need to do is 1) pay attention to where the argument seems to be going, and 2) complete the argument in a conservative and sensible fashion.

If you haven't done so already, please read the argument now and see if you can predict what a sensible completion of the argument might be. In the next paragraph, I'll tell you where I think it's going.

The first two sentences of this argument introduce an analogy between "a century" and "a life." Now, I personally think this is total crap. One is an arbitrary period of time, and one is a person. Superficially, you can make an analogy between just about any two things, even when in reality they are in no way similar. So this analogy sucks, and I'm not buying it. But, I'm going to let go of that because that's just not the point. The point is this: If you were forced to use this crappy analogy, what could you use it for? Maybe this is like being an attorney with a useless client or a very annoying case... sometimes you have to make the best of what you've got.

The argument concludes with "So just as people in their last years spend much time looking back on the events of their life, people at a century's end _____." Since the argument said that a century is like a life, I guess the blank has to be filled in with a similarity between a century and a life. So I guess what this moron was going to say is "Just as people spend their last years looking back at the events of their life, people at century's end look back at the events of the past century." Wow. That's not exactly earth-shattering, is it? But who cares—that's where the argument was going, and it's justified if we accept the crappy analogy (which we must, because it's all we have to work with). I think this prediction is going to be very close to the correct answer.

A) Not what we're looking for. This would be a good answer if it said "reminisce about the century."

B) What? Um... this definitely happens in real life, but it isn't what the argument was talking about.

C) No. This probably also sometimes happens, but it's not what the argument was talking about. If you chose either B or C, you probably weren't paying close enough attention to where the argument was actually going.

D) This didn't immediately look like a match to me, but "history of the century" is, of course, very similar to "the events of the past century." This is probably the correct answer.

E) This would be the correct answer if the facts said that old people tend to reflect on how they could have avoided unfortunate events in their lives. But the facts didn't say that, it just said people "look back." Remorse wasn't mentioned.

So D is our answer.

One final note on this type of question: You have really got to predict this answer in advance, *before* looking at the answer choices. The answer choices are not your friend. They are mostly tricks, traps, and time-wasters. If you don't make a prediction, then several of the answers are probably going to look reasonable to you and you're going to 1) get confused and 2) waste a ton of time. Slow down and invest a little time up front. You'll end up going much faster overall, and with much greater accuracy.

Strategy of Argumentation

Strategy of Argumentation questions present an argument, and then ask you to pick an answer choice that describes the strategy that the argument employed.

Example Question Stems:
• Which one of the following most accurately describes the method of reasoning used in the argument?
• Which of the following most accurately describes the role played in the argument by X
• X undermines the conclusion of the argument by

June **2007**
Section **2**
Question **20**

Gamba: Muñoz claims that the Southwest Hopeville Neighbors Association overwhelmingly opposes the new water system, citing this as evidence of citywide opposition. The association did pass a resolution opposing the new water system, but only 25 of 350 members voted, with 10 in favor of the system. Furthermore, the 15 opposing votes represent far less than 1 percent of Hopeville's population. One should not assume that so few votes represent the view of the majority of Hopeville's residents.

Of the following, which one most accurately describes Gamba's strategy of argumentation?

A) questioning a conclusion based on the results of a vote, on the grounds that people with certain views are more likely to vote
B) questioning a claim supported by statistical data by arguing that statistical data can be manipulated to support whatever view the interpreter wants to support
C) attempting to refute an argument by showing that, contrary to what has been claimed, the truth of the premises does not guarantee the truth of the conclusion
D) criticizing a view on the grounds that the view is based on evidence that is in principle impossible to disconfirm
E) attempting to cast doubt on a conclusion by claiming that the statistical sample on which the conclusion is based is too small to be dependable

Let's try to figure out what's going on in this question. Gamba is the speaker, and he's trying to argue with Muñoz. Muñoz claims that since the Southwest Hopeville Neighbors Association "overwhelmingly opposes" the new water system, there must be citywide opposition as well. Gamba says not so fast—not enough of the Neighbors Association members voted, and some of those who did vote actually voted for the plan. Since there wasn't a big enough sample, Gamba says, we can't make any conclusion about the entire population. This makes sense to me—I think Gamba's logic is reasonable.

The question stem says: "Of the following, which one most accurately describes Gamba's strategy of argumentation?" I might not be able to exactly predict the wording that the testmakers will use to describe the strategy employed by Gamba, but I'll take a crack at it: I think Gamba claimed there was too small a sample to make any final conclusion. Let's see if we can find that, or something similar to that, in the answer choices.

Note: You must be hyper-critical of the answer choices on a Strategy of Argumentation question. You must, at a minimum, choose an answer that describes a strategy actually employed by Gamba. So if an answer choice says Gamba did anything that Gamba did not actually do, then it can't possibly be the answer.

A) No, Gamba didn't ever claim that some people are more likely to vote than others. This is surely true in real life, but that's not the angle Gamba took. This is out.
B) No, Gamba didn't ever claim that the data could have been "manipulated." This might also be true in real life, but this is also not the angle Gamba took. No way.
C) I like this answer. Gamba doesn't disagree with Muñoz's evidence—he seems to agree that the Neighbors Association did vote in the way Muñoz said it voted—but he disagrees with Muñoz's interpretation of that evidence. Muñoz thinks his evidence means something, whereas Gamba thinks the evidence, even if valid, is too small a sample to draw any real conclusion. I'm 95% sure that this will be the correct answer.
D) No, Gamba didn't ever claim that Muñoz's evidence would be impossible to disprove. This would be the answer if Gamba had said "your premises are untestable"—but Gamba didn't say that. So this is out.
E) Whoops! I was in love with C, but having read E I'm in a bit of a pickle. This answer choice is exactly what I was looking for. So I have to reread C, even more critically this time, and see if I can find fault with it. And I think I can. Answer C says "contrary to what has been claimed, the truth of the premises does not guarantee the truth of the conclusion." The problem with this is that Muñoz did not guarantee that there was citywide opposition; Muñoz only cited the study as evidence of citywide opposition. This is a fine shade of meaning, but I think C goes a step too far in alleging that Muñoz said something he didn't necessarily say.

Since I know for sure that Gamba did claim the sample was too small, and since E describes exactly that, **the answer is E**.

Note: It's critical that you read all five answer choices on the Logical Reasoning. I really thought C was the answer, and it would have been very tempting to try to cleverly shave off a few seconds by skipping D and E. Had I done so, I would have not-so-cleverly shaved one point off my score.

Matching Pattern

Matching Pattern questions give you an argument, and then ask you to choose an answer that most closely matches the strategy of argumentation used by the given argument. These are among the hardest and most time consuming of all LSAT questions, and should be skipped by test-takers who are not currently scoring 150 or higher. Harvest the lower-hanging fruit first.

Example Question Stems:
• The pattern of reasoning in which one of the following arguments is most similar to the argument above?
• Which one of the following arguments is most similar in its pattern of reasoning to the argument above?
• The reasoning in the argument above is most closely paralleled by the argument that

> June **2007**
> Section **3**
> Question **20**

We should accept the proposal to demolish the old train station, because the local historical society, which vehemently opposes this, is dominated by people who have no commitment to long-term economic well-being. Preserving old buildings creates an impediment to new development, which is critical to economic health.

The flawed reasoning exhibited by the argument above is most similar to that exhibited by which one of the following arguments?

A) Our country should attempt to safeguard works of art that it deems to possess national cultural significance. These works might not be recognized as such by all taxpayers, or even all critics. Nevertheless, our country ought to expend whatever money is needed to procure all such works as they become available.

B) Documents of importance to local heritage should be properly preserved and archived for the sake of future generations. For, if even one of these documents is damaged or lost, the integrity of the historical record as a whole will be damaged.

C) You should have your hair cut no more than once a month. After all, beauticians suggest that their customers have their hair cut twice a month, and they do this as a way of generating more business for themselves.

D) The committee should endorse the plan to postpone construction of the new expressway. Many residents of the neighborhoods that would be affected are fervently opposed to that construction, and the committee is obligated to avoid alienating those residents.

E) One should not borrow even small amounts of money unless it is absolutely necessary. Once one borrows a few dollars, the interest starts to accumulate. The longer one takes to repay, the more one ends up owing, and eventually a small debt has become a large one.

This question has a swear word near the beginning. Well, maybe not according to your mom, but if you've read any of my other books, taken my class, or have otherwise been listening to me yell about the LSAT long enough, the word should go off like an F-bomb every time you read it. Hint: The dirty word starts with "S."

To an LSAT expert, the word that jumps off the page in the above argument is the word "should." Every time you read the word "should," I want you to immediately think, "Don't fucking tell me what I, or we, or anybody else 'should' do." (This is for the LSAT only, by the way. You're likely to lose some friends if you take this too wide.)

The word "should" almost always indicates the conclusion of an LSAT argument, and that argument is almost always bullshit. An aversion to the word "should" will help you criticize the argument. Being critical leads to understanding. Understanding leads to correct answers.

The argument tries to convince us that we should demolish the old train station. Since we're skeptical of being told what we "should" do, we're going to demand some reasons. If you're going to tell us what we "should" do, then you better explain why. So, what are the reasons that the argument provides? I see two reasons, one better than the other:

1) "The local historical society, which vehemently opposes this, is dominated by people who have no commitment to long-term economic well-being." This is an "ad hominem" attack against some people who disagree with the desired action, and this would never be acceptable on the LSAT. Even a broken clock is right twice a day! Simply saying "this clock is broken" doesn't prove that the clock isn't giving you the correct time. Let's see if the other reason is any better.

2) "Preserving old buildings creates an impediment to new development, which is critical to economic health." This is a better reason, but it assumes that we give a shit about "new development" and "economic health." What if we don't care about development and economic health? If we don't, then why wouldn't we preserve the old train station?

So the argument presents two reasons, one completely bogus and the other incomplete, in support of a conclusion telling us what we should do. We understand the argument!

Now we can look at the question: "The flawed reasoning exhibited by the argument above is most similar to that exhibited by which one of the following arguments?"

OK, this shouldn't be too tough. Let's look for an answer choice that presents two reasons in support of a conclusion that tells us what we should do. Ideally, the two reasons will be an ad hominem attack and a reason that requires an assumption. That's two flaws. A perfect answer would have both of them.

A) This argument looks circular to me. "We should safeguard works of art... because we ought to." I don't see an ad hominem attack here. And I don't see a reason that requires an assumption. The argument is certainly flawed, but I don't think it's flawed in the same way as the given argument.

B) This argument doesn't have an ad hominem attack, but it does require the assumption that we care about "the integrity of the historical record as a whole." Let's look for something better.

C) This argument does contain an ad hominem attack (those dirty beauticians are trying to rip you off!) and it further requires an assumption that you care about minimizing the amount of business you give to beauticians. I like it.

D) Nah. There's no ad hominem attack here, and there's no assumption.

E) There's no ad hominem attack here, but at least there's an assumption (that we care about avoiding large debts). but that's not enough when C is in the ballgame.

Our answer is C, because it contains both of the flaws we were looking for.

Matching Flaw

Matching Flaw questions present you with a flawed argument, and ask you to choose an answer that exhibits the same logical flaw. It is critical to know what flaw you're looking for before looking at the answer choices, or else all five answers might sound good to you.

Example Question Stems:
• Which one of the following arguments exhibits flawed reasoning most similar to that exhibited by the argument above?
• Which one of the following exhibits both of the logical flaws exhibited in the arguments above?
• The flawed pattern of reasoning in which of the following most closely resembles the flawed pattern of reasoning in the actor's argument?

> June **2007**
> Section **2**
> Question **2**

All Labrador retrievers bark a great deal. All Saint Bernards bark infrequently. Each of Rosa's dogs is a cross between a Labrador retriever and a Saint Bernard. Therefore, Rosa's dogs are moderate barkers.

Which one of the following uses flawed reasoning that most closely resembles the flawed reasoning used in the argument above?

A) All students who study diligently make good grades. But some students who do not study diligently also make good grades. Jane studies somewhat diligently. Therefore, Jane makes somewhat good grades.

B) All type A chemicals are extremely toxic to human beings. All type B chemicals are nontoxic to human beings. This household cleaner is a mixture of a type A chemical and a type B chemical. Therefore, this household cleaner is moderately toxic.

C) All students at Hanson School live in Green County. All students at Edwards School live in Winn County. Members of the Perry family attend both Hanson and Edwards. Therefore, some members of the Perry family live in Green County and some live in Winn County.

D) All transcriptionists know shorthand. All engineers know calculus. Bob has worked both as a transcriptionist and as an engineer. Therefore, Bob knows both shorthand and calculus.

E) All of Kenisha's dresses are very well made. All of Connie's dresses are very badly made. Half of the dresses in this closet are very well made, and half of them are very badly made. Therefore, half of the dresses in this closet are Kenisha's and half of them are Connie's.

The argument presented in Question 2 starts with a fact about Labs (they all bark a lot). Then it presents a fact about Saint Bernards (they all rarely bark). Then it says Rosa's dogs are all Lab/St. Bernard mixes. Then, predictably, it makes a dumbass conclusion about how often Rosa's dogs bark. Can you tell me why this argument is bullshit?

It really doesn't matter here whether the conclusion says the dogs bark all the time, or never bark, or "bark moderately." The problem is that crosses can have different characteristics from either of two purebreds. Since Rosa's dogs are crosses, we really can't make any conclusion about them. The facts only give us evidence about purebreds.

The argument here is just like saying "all monkeys are good climbers but bad swimmers, and all fish are good swimmers but bad climbers, so this cross between a monkey and a fish will be a moderate swimmer and a moderate climber. Does that make sense? Um, no. I'm not a biologist, nor does the LSAT require me to be. But common sense says we just can't predict how such a hybrid would turn out. This is the same problem with the logic about Rosa's dogs.

The Question asks us to find an answer choice that demonstrates a similar flawed pattern of reasoning. So the correct answer must be 1) flawed and 2) flawed in the same way. Before you go on to the answer choices, it's probably useful to see if you can come up with a similar example like my monkey/fish example above. Give it at least a few seconds, then take a deep breath and move on to the answers.

A) My problem with this answer choice is the word "some" in the second sentence. The argument about Rosa's dogs never used "some"... it was all or nothing. So I'm very skeptical that this will turn out to be the correct answer. Remember that 80% of the answer choices are, by definition, incorrect. Start with the presumption that the answer choice you are reading at any moment is probably not the answer. The instant something about an answer choice smells fishy, we should move on. We can always come back if necessary, but we should only reconsider this answer after reading all the other choices and deciding that none of them are any good.

B) This looks perfect to me. Type A is very toxic, but Type B is nontoxic, therefore a blend of the two will be "moderately toxic"? How on earth would we possibly know that to be true? It's possible that the mix could be either very toxic, or not toxic at all. (Just like Rosa's dogs might bark constantly, or never.) This is a bad argument, and it's bad in the same way as the given argument. This looks like a great answer.

C) There's no flaw here. If all the facts are true, then the conclusion must also be true. Remember we're looking for a flawed answer choice. So this can't be our answer.

D) This might be flawed, in that Bob could be 90 years old and maybe he has forgotten both shorthand and calculus. Anyway, even if this is flawed it isn't similarly flawed, because there's nothing here about blending two things together and having an outcome that is a hybrid of the two initial things. B is still the best answer by far.

E) This is definitely flawed, because there are surely a million people who make great dresses besides Kenisha, and a million people who make shitty dresses besides Connie. But again there is no "mixing" going on here.

I am very confident that **B is our answer**.

Analytical Reasoning (Logic Games)

(Excerpted from *Breaking the LSAT*)

On the logic games, just like the rest of the LSAT, you have to slow down in order to speed up. First, the good news: Hardly anybody completes all four games. So your goal here is to slow down and focus on accuracy.

Unlike the rest of the LSAT, where often you have to pick the best of a bad bunch of answers, every question on the logic games has a single, objectively correct answer. There is no picking the "best" answer on the logic games. Rather, there are four terrible, wrong answers that you hate and one perfect answer that you should love. Focus on answering the questions with 100% certainty. For starters, see if you can just get every answer right on a single game. If you can do this in 35 minutes, you're on the right track. Next, see if you can do two games perfectly in 35 minutes. Believe it or not, that would put you well ahead of the average test taker. If you can do three games perfectly, you'll be in the top 10 percent. But you have to walk before you can run.

There are two basic operations on LSAT Logic Games: Putting things in order, and putting things in groups. (Harder games will do a combination of both, but for now we'll start with the basics.) In this section, we'll walk through one of each type. Turn the page, and let's get started.

Putting Things in Order

June **2007**
Section **1**
Game **1**

A company employee generates a series of five-digit product codes in accordance with the following rules:

- The codes use the digits 0, 1, 2, 3, and 4, and no others.
- Each digit occurs exactly once in any code.
- The second digit has a value exactly twice that of the first digit.
- The value of the third digit is less than the value of the fifth digit.

Do the "if..." questions first

All credit for this technique goes to my Thinking LSAT Podcast co-host Ben Olson. (You met him in the foreword.) Ben taught me this tip after I'd already been teaching the LSAT for years; as an LSAT teacher, I never stop learning about this test. The awesome thing about this technique is that when it helps, it helps a lot. You'll see me employ it throughout the book. Here goes:

After doing the list question (usually the first question in every game), you'll notice that I then do all the questions that start with "If..." before circling back and doing everything else. I do this because 1) the "if" questions are often easier and 2) sometimes you can use the work you do on the "if" questions to eliminate wrong answers on other questions. Quick example. Let's say there's a rule that Clown X must get out of the clown car immediately before Clown Y. And let's say there's a question that starts out "if X gets out fifth, blah blah blah." In that case, Y obviously gets out sixth, right? Too easy. Of course, that doesn't mean that Y always goes sixth, because the "if" rule is only active for that one question. (The "if" rules do not accumulate, or apply to any other questions.) However, it does mean that in some cases, Y does go sixth. Y cannot be prohibited from going sixth, otherwise, the question itself would be invalid. So if another question asks something like "which of the following cannot go sixth," we would know right away, based on the "if" question we did earlier, that Y cannot be the answer for this question. Sometimes you can eliminate two, or three, or even all four wrong answers on a question like this by using the work you've already done on the list and "if" questions.

If that example doesn't make it immediately clear, don't panic. You'll see plenty of examples later in the book. For now, just notice that I'm doing the list question first (if there is one), then the "if" questions, then all the rest. This will make heaps more sense with lots and lots of practice. If it doesn't, blame Ben. ;)

Game Setup (Questions 1-5)   (Excerpted from *The Logic Games Playbook*)

Some games, including this one, can be split into two templates or "worlds." You don't have to split it, but the best gamers will do so from time to time. Experts aggressively look for opportunities to execute an attack like the one you're about to see. When it works, it can bring a game to its knees. This game, which happens to be the first game in the June 2007 LSAT, isn't really all that challenging. But two worlds make it even easier, giving us more time for the harder games that come after it.

A company employee generates a series of five-digit product codes in accordance with the following rules:

- The codes use the digits 0, 1, 2, 3, and 4, and no others.
- Each digit occurs exactly once in any code.
- The second digit has a value exactly twice that of the first digit.
- The value of the third digit is less than the value of the fifth digit.

The rule that allows for this "two worlds" approach is the third one: "The second digit has a value exactly twice that of the first digit." Because our digits are only 0, 1, 2, 3, and 4, there are only two ways to have the second digit be twice the first:

$$
\begin{array}{ccccc}
1 & 2 & \underline{\quad} & \underline{\quad} & \underline{\quad} \\
\\
2 & 4 & \underline{\quad} & \underline{\quad} & \underline{\quad}
\end{array}
$$

That realization alone is enough to crush this game, but we can go further. To deal with the last rule—that the third spot is less than the fifth—we can draw arrows connecting the third and fifth spots, with little "less than" signs between them:

In our first world, the three remaining digits are 0, 3, and 4. The "less than" rule prevents 4 from going in the third spot and 0 from going in the fifth spot. That means the third spot must be 0 or 3, and the fifth spot must be 3 or 4.

In our second world, on the other hand, the three remaining digits are 0, 1, and 3, which are also constrained by the "less than" rule. Because 3 can't go third and 0 can't go fifth, 0 or 1 must be third and 1 or 3 must be fifth:

As it turns out, this game has very little flexibility. All conceivable scenarios are captured by our two worlds; there are no other possibilities. It's time to attack the questions.

QUESTION 1

If the last digit of an acceptable product code is 1, it must be true that the

(A) first digit is 2
(B) second digit is 0
(C) third digit is 3
(D) fourth digit is 4
(E) fourth digit is 0

The only way to make the last digit 1 would be in our second world. So let's use that world and incorporate the new rule:

| 2 | 4 | ___ | ___ | 1 |

By the way, we do not—under any circumstances—write this new sketch on top of our original diagram. We need to keep our original diagram pristine to answer the other questions. The new condition "fifth digit is 1" applies to only question 1, so we're making a new mini-diagram to solve this question.

And now that we have this diagram, we can go further. Given that the third digit must be less than the fifth, 0 must go third, which forces 3 into the fourth spot:

| 2 | 4 | 0 | 3 | 1 |

It shouldn't be too tough to answer the question from here. We're asked to find what must be true.

A) Yes, the first digit is two. We went a couple steps further than necessary to solve this question, but that's going to happen sometimes. And it's not a wasted effort; we might return to this diagram when solving a later question. Let's just skim through B-E before we pick A.
B) No, the second digit is 4.
C) No, the third digit is 0.
D) No, the fourth digit is 3.
E) No, the fourth digit is 3.

Our answer is A.

QUESTION 3

If the third digit of an acceptable product code is not 0, which one of the following must be true?

(A) The second digit of the product code is 2.
(B) The third digit of the product code is 3.
(C) The fourth digit of the product code is 0.
(D) The fifth digit of the product code is 3.
(E) The fifth digit of the product code is 1.

Doing the "if" questions first, we'll skip question 2 for now. For question 3, we look at our two original worlds and realize that the third digit doesn't have to be 0 in either one. So we'll sketch two mini-diagrams for this question:

1	2	3	___	___
2	4	1	___	___

Because the fifth digit has to be greater than the third, that forces 4 into the last spot for our first scenario and 3 into the last spot for our second scenario. We can then fill in the only remaining number in both worlds, which happens to be 0:

1	2	3	0	4
2	4	1	0	3

Because we're asked to find a must be true, the correct answer must be true in both worlds.

Looking at our two scenarios, the only spot that's the same in both is the fourth one, which is 0. To save time, we scan the answers for 0 and quickly notice that answer C is the only one. That doesn't mean it's correct, of course. We have to read the entire answer. But doing so does confirm that it is correct.

As you get better at the games, you can move on. But for now, let's scan the rest of these answers to be sure we didn't miss anything:

A) No, this is only true in our first scenario.
B) No, this is only true in our first scenario.
C) Yes, this is true in both scenarios.
D) No, this is only true in our second scenario.
E) No, this isn't true in either scenario.

Our answer is C, after all.

QUESTION 2

Which one of the following must be true about any acceptable product code?

(A) The digit 1 appears in some position before the digit 2.
(B) The digit 1 appears in some position before the digit 3.
(C) The digit 2 appears in some position before the digit 3.
(D) The digit 3 appears in some position before the digit 0.
(E) The digit 4 appears in some position before the digit 3.

Having exhausted the "if" questions, we return to question 2. We're asked to find something that must be true, and this means must be true in every valid scenario, which now includes not only our two original worlds, but also the diagrams we drew for questions 1 and 3. Let's see.

A) No, this doesn't have to be true in the world that starts 2 4 _ _ _.
B) No, this didn't happen in our diagram for question 1.
C) Yep, our two templates start with 1 2 and 2 4. In both scenarios, digit 2 is in either the first or second spot and digit 3 has yet to appear. To be 100% sure, let's scan D and E.
D) No, this didn't happen in question 1.
E) This didn't happen in our first diagram for question 3.

Our answer is C, because it's always true in every scenario.

QUESTION 4

Any of the following pairs could be the third and fourth digits, respectively, of an acceptable product code, EXCEPT:

(A) 0, 1
(B) 0, 3
(C) 1, 0
(D) 3, 0
(E) 3, 4

We're looking for something that won't work in the third and fourth spots. So anything that will work in the third and fourth spots, in any of our existing scenarios, is out.

A) Haven't seen this happen yet. Let's leave it for now, and see if we can eliminate everything else. If we can, then we can choose this answer without even testing it.
B) This happened in our diagram for question 1. So this is out.
C) This happened in our second diagram for question 3. Also out.
D) This happened in our first diagram for question 3. Out.
E) Haven't seen this happen yet either. Let's quickly test A and E, and see which one won't work.

For answer A (_ _ 0 1 _) to work, we have to use the scenario that starts with 2 4:

$$ \underline{\;2\;} \quad \underline{\;4\;} \quad \underline{\;0\;} \quad \underline{\;1\;} \quad \underline{\;3\;} $$

That seems to work, so I bet the answer is E. Let's prove it.
   For answer E (_ _ 3 4 _) to work, we have to use the scenario that starts with 1 2. Like this:

$$ \underline{\;1\;} \quad \underline{\;2\;} \quad \underline{\;3\;} \quad \underline{\;4\;} \quad \underline{\;0\;} $$

But in that scenario, we're breaking the rule that says the fifth digit has to be greater than the third. So 3, 4 isn't an acceptable scenario. We'll cross that scenario out, so we don't mistakenly assume that it's valid later.

Our answer is E.

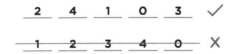

QUESTION 5

Which one of the following must be true about any acceptable product code?

(A) There is exactly one digit between the digit 0 and the digit 1.
(B) There is exactly one digit between the digit 1 and the digit 2.
(C) There are at most two digits between the digit 1 and the digit 3.
(D) There are at most two digits between the digit 2 and the digit 3.
(E) There are at most two digits between the digit 2 and the digit 4.

Again, we're asked to identify something that must be true, and again this means something that is true in all scenarios. So we should be able to do a process of elimination here, knocking out any answer choices that were not true in any valid scenario.

A) This wasn't true in our first diagram for question 3.
B) This wasn't true in our diagram for question 1.
C) This is true in all of our special diagrams, but in our original first world—the one that starts with 1 & 2—it looks like 3 could have been last, which would violate this condition.
D) This wasn't true in our first scenario for question 4.
E) This is true in all of our mini-diagrams, and looking at our two worlds, it's always going to be true. In the first world, 2 is second, so even if 4 is last, there are still only two digits separating them. In the second world, 2 and 4 are right next to each other, so 2 and 4 are never going to be separated by more than two digits. This is our answer.

Our answer is E.

This game tends to throw some LSAT students for a loop simply because it has numbers and the "twice than" rule, which makes students' math-phobia kick in. But you couldn't have graduated from third grade, much less high school, and much less college, without this level of mathematical proficiency. Don't let it get in your head—it's an easy game as long as you don't panic.

We can say the same thing about many, many logic games. As professional LSAT teachers, we frequently hear our students say, "You make it look so easy!" By the time we're done with you, our hope is to convince you that the reason we make it look so easy is that it actually is easy.

Putting Things in Groups

> June **2007**
> Section **1**
> Game **4**

There are exactly three recycling centers in Rivertown: Center 1, Center 2, and Center 3. Exactly five kinds of material are recycled at these recycling centers: glass, newsprint, plastic, tin, and wood. Each recycling center recycles at least two but no more than three of these kinds of material. The following conditions must hold:

- Any recycling center that recycles wood also recycles newsprint.
- Every kind of material that Center 2 recycles is also recycled at Center 1.
- Only one of the recycling centers recycles plastic, and that recycling center does not recycle glass.

Game Setup (Questions 18-23)

(Excerpted from *The Logic Games Playbook*)

This game is quite a bit tougher, at least on its surface. Maybe the questions will turn out to be easy; we never know until we get there. But from a setup standpoint, this one seems a bit trickier. Here's how I see this one:

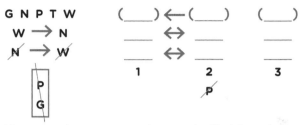

The lines without parentheses are spots that must be filled. So each group has two spots without parentheses and one spot with. Since anything that's in group 2 must also be in group 1, we have double arrows going between the mandatory spots in groups 1 and 2. For the optional spot, the arrow there only goes one way. If group 2 has three types of materials, then whatever that third thing is has to go in group 1 as well. But group 1 can have a random third thing in it that doesn't match group 2, as long as group 2 has only two types of materials.

Note also that we've made one inference; since anything in group 2 has to also be in group 1, and since plastic can only go once, this means that plastic can't be in group 2. (It can, however, be in group 1 as long as it's the third, optional, material.)

Beyond that, it seems like there's quite a bit of flexibility here. So rather than over-complicate things, let's dive into the questions.

QUESTION 18

Which one of the following could be an accurate account of all the kinds of material recycled at each recycling center in Rivertown?

(A) Center 1: newsprint, plastic, wood; Center 2: newsprint, wood; Center 3: glass, tin, wood

(B) Center 1: glass, newsprint, tin; Center 2: glass, newsprint, tin; Center 3: newsprint, plastic, wood

(C) Center 1: glass, newsprint, wood; Center 2: glass, newsprint, tin; Center 3: plastic, tin

(D) Center 1: glass, plastic, tin; Center 2: glass, tin; Center 3: newsprint, wood

(E) Center 1: newsprint, plastic, wood; Center 2: newsprint, plastic, wood; Center 3: glass, newsprint, tin

List question—let's do the process of elimination.

• If W → N, this gets rid of A.
• Anything in group 2 has to be in group 1. This gets rid of C.
• P can only go once. This gets rid of E.
• P and G can't go together. This gets rid of D.

Our answer is B, because it can't be anything else.

QUESTION 20

If Center 2 recycles three kinds of material, then which one of the following kinds of material must Center 3 recycle?

(A) glass
(B) newsprint
(C) plastic
(D) tin
(E) wood

(Skipping 19 to tackle the "if" questions first.) No need to do a diagram here; the answer is "plastic." As we noted earlier, plastic can never go in group 2, and can only go in group 1 if it's the optional, third material in that group. But if group 2 has three things, then P can't go in group 1 either. Our inference really helped us out there.

So P has to go in group 3, **and that's our answer: C.**

QUESTION 21

If each recycling center in Rivertown recycles exactly three kinds of material, then which one of the following could be true?

(A) Only Center 2 recycles glass.
(B) Only Center 3 recycles newsprint.
(C) Only Center 1 recycles plastic.
(D) Only Center 3 recycles tin.
(E) Only Center 1 recycles wood.

Here, we'll make a diagram. The steps are basically these:

• P must go in group 3, and nowhere else, for the reasons we discussed previously.
• G can't go in group 3, because P is there.
• N must go in both groups 1 and 2, because without N you can't have W, and without N, W, and P you wouldn't be able to have three types of material.

The diagram looks like this:

Hopefully that's enough to answer the question. We're looking for something that could be true. Let's see:

A) No, because everything in groups 1 and 2 has to match.
B) No, because N is already in both groups 1 and 2.
C) No, because P is already in group 3.
D) This seems possible. If we can get rid of E, this will be our answer.
E) No, because everything in groups 1 and 2 has to match.

Our answer is D, because it's the only one that will work.

Note that we didn't even bother testing it; if we're certain that the answer can't be A, B, C, or E, then the answer must be D. Any time you can shave on this test will help you answer the tougher questions. It's worth it.

QUESTION 22

If Center 3 recycles glass, then which one of the following kinds of material must Center 2 recycle?

(A) glass
(B) newsprint
(C) plastic
(D) tin
(E) wood

Again, a new diagram is in order. The steps are basically:

- If center 3 has G, it can't have P.
- The only other place P can possibly go is in the optional spot for group 1.
- Therefore, group 2 can only have two materials (no optional material).
- Group 1, since it has P, can't have G.
- This leaves only W, N, and T for the two remaining spots in group 1. Without N, you can't have W; this would leave a shortage of materials in group 1. So group 1 has to have N.
- If group 1 has N, then group 2 must have N as well.

Here's the diagram:

P   X   ___
    ⟷
___   ___   ___

N ⟷ N   G
1   2   3
G̶   P̶

We're asked for something that must be in center 2, and the last step above got us there. Center 2 must have newsprint.

Our answer is B.

QUESTION 23

If Center 1 is the only recycling center that recycles wood, then which one of the following could be a complete and accurate list of the kinds of material that one of the recycling centers recycles?

(A) plastic, tin
(B) newsprint, wood
(C) newsprint, tin
(D) glass, wood
(E) glass, tin

Again, a new diagram. The steps are these:

• If group 1 is the only group with W, then that must be the optional material in group 1.
• Therefore group 2 has no optional material.
• If group 1 has W, it must also have N.
• If group 1 has N, then group 2 must as well.
• Group 2 can't have W or P.
• Because P can't go anywhere else, it must go in group 3.
• With P in group 3, G can't go there.

Here's the step that almost everyone, including an LSAT professional, will miss. The rules say "exactly five kinds of materials are recycled." It hasn't come up so far, but this means that we do need to use each kind of material at least once. If that's true, then both group 1 and 2 are going to have to have G.
For the same reason, Group 3 now has to have T.

Here's the finished diagram:

W		X		(___)
G	⟷	G		T
N	⟷	N		P
1		2		3
P̸		P̸		W̸
		W̸		G̸

We're looking for a list that could be the complete list of materials recycled in one of the groups. We can probably eliminate a lot of wrong answers here, hopefully four of them.

A) This looks like it might be possible in group 3. Let's not test it though; let's just see if we can get rid of B-E.
B) No, this can't be the complete list in any of the groups. Group 1 must have three things, not two. Group 2 and 3 can't have W, if group 1 is the only group allowed to have W.
C) No, this is impossible. This is the answer choice that's very hard to eliminate if you forget that you have to use all five materials at least once.
D) No, this won't work.
E) Nope.

Our answer is A, because B-E won't work.

QUESTION 19

Which one of the following is a complete and accurate list of the recycling centers in Rivertown any one of which could recycle plastic?

(A) Center 1 only
(B) Center 3 only
(C) Center 1, Center 2
(D) Center 1, Center 3
(E) Center 1, Center 2, Center 3

We predicted this one in our initial setup. The only place P can go is groups 1 and 3. If that's an answer choice, it's our answer.

Yep. **Our answer is D.**

These few pages in this tiny book contain 100 percent of everything I know about the LSAT's Reading Comprehension. There's simply not that much to say. My philosophy on RC includes no diagramming, no underlining, no highlighting, no note-taking, and no silly trademarked acronyms to memorize.

It's a simple two-step process, y'all: Step one: Read. Step two: Comprehend. The two steps are performed simultaneously.

I'm not being a smartass; this is my professional opinion. I simply don't know anybody who's good at the LSAT who actually uses any of the overcomplicated RC "strategies" that are taught in a typical LSAT class. If you read carefully, you will comprehend. If you don't comprehend, then you didn't read carefully enough. It's not much more complicated than that.

Lawyers read—a lot—and the LSAT wants to know whether you've got what it takes. Half of this battle is beyond your control. Native English speakers have a big advantage, of course. If you spent your incredibly dorky childhood reading stacks of books for pleasure, like I did, that pays off too. I hate to break it to you, but no amount of strategy is going to level the playing field here. We can't change history.

But the other half of this battle comes down to determination. Can you force yourself to pay attention? Can you stay awake, stay engaged, and understand what you're reading? Or will you let your eyes glaze over and succumb to daydreaming? The LSAT is trying to get you to space out by presenting you with poorly written passages on boring-ass topics. See how nice it is outside? Don't you want to go outside and play? I heard someone say there's free beer out there... If you're a lawyer, you will resist this siren song. Reading poorly written, boring-ass shit is exactly what lawyers do. This is what you're signing up for, so you better

Reading Comprehension

get used to it! No, I do not want to drink a beer outside in the sunshine. I'm a lawyer, goddamn it, and I have important (boring) reading to do.

Read actively! The passage might not seem very titillating in the early going, but if you fake interest at the beginning, you might find that you actually become interested. I'm talking about active, aggressive engagement with the ideas. What you're going for, more than anything, is the author's main point. Ask the author, repeatedly, as you work your way through the passage: Why are you wasting my time with this? What are you getting at? What message are you trying to deliver? The closer you pay attention, the more you'll understand. RC doesn't suck nearly as much when you actually understand what the speaker is talking about, and that's the entire point.

Another tip for active reading: Engaged readers naturally make frequent predictions as they read. You just said ABC... I bet you're eventually going to say XYZ. The point of these predictions isn't to be right or wrong; it's to make sure you're staying awake. After a couple sentences, or the first paragraph, stop and make a prediction. If you can't come up with anything, then you have no idea what you've been reading and you should probably start over. Better to start over after two sentences than after the entire passage. As you get deeper into the passage, you'll find out whether your prediction was right or wrong.

The good news is that it doesn't matter either way. If you thought they were going to say XYZ but you end up noticing that they actually said RST instead, that means you understood. Like making a beer bet on a football game you don't give a shit about, you pay better attention to the game whether or not you win.

Reading Comprehension

In tracing the changing face of the Irish
landscape, scholars have traditionally relied primarily
on evidence from historical documents. However, such
documentary sources provide a fragmentary record at
(5)   best. Reliable accounts are very scarce for many parts
of Ireland prior to the seventeenth century, and many
of the relevant documents from the sixteenth and
seventeenth centuries focus selectively on matters
relating to military or commercial interests.

(10)   Studies of fossilized pollen grains preserved in
peats and lake muds provide an additional means of
investigating vegetative landscape change. Details of
changes in vegetation resulting from both human
activities and natural events are reflected in the kinds
(15)   and quantities of minute pollen grains that become
trapped in sediments. Analysis of samples can identify
which kinds of plants produced the preserved pollen
grains and when they were deposited, and in many
cases the findings can serve to supplement or correct
(20)   the documentary record.

For example, analyses of samples from Long
Lough in County Down have revealed significant
patterns of cereal-grain pollen beginning by about 400
A.D. The substantial clay content of the soil in this part
(25)   of Down makes cultivation by primitive tools difficult.
Historians thought that such soils were not tilled to
any significant extent until the introduction of the
moldboard plough to Ireland in the seventh century
A.D. Because cereal cultivation would have required

(30) tilling of the soil, the pollen evidence indicates that these soils must indeed have been successfully tilled before the introduction of the new plough.

Another example concerns flax cultivation in County Down, one of the great linen-producing areas of
(35) Ireland during the eighteenth century. Some aspects of linen production in Down are well documented, but the documentary record tells little about the cultivation of flax, the plant from which linen is made, in that area. The record of eighteenth-century linen
(40) production in Down, together with the knowledge that flax cultivation had been established in Ireland centuries before that time, led some historians to surmise that this plant was being cultivated in Down before the eighteenth century. But pollen analyses
(45) indicate that this is not the case; flax pollen was found only in deposits laid down since the eighteenth century.

It must be stressed, though, that there are limits to the ability of the pollen record to reflect the vegetative
(50) history of the landscape. For example, pollen analyses cannot identify the species, but only the genus or family, of some plants. Among these is madder, a cultivated dye plant of historical importance in Ireland. Madder belongs to a plant family that also comprises
(55) various native weeds, including goosegrass. If madder pollen were present in a deposit it would be indistinguishable from that of uncultivated native species.

Fake It 'Til You Make It (Questions 23-27)

Remember our battle cry: *Why are you wasting my time with this, goddamn it?!?*

This passage starts off articulating a problem with Irish history. Documents regarding the vegetative landscape are scarce, and fragmentary, and focus on military/commercial interests which, presumably, don't tell the full story. At the end of the first paragraph, I can predict that the speaker is probably going to give us some solution to this problem—otherwise, why would she be talking about it?

The second paragraph proves this prediction right. The author seems optimistic about the study of fossilized pollen grains as a way of supplementing historical documents. Apparently, studying fossilized pollen grains give us information about what plants were growing where, and when. This does seem like it might be useful; if, for example, corn suddenly started being grown in some certain part of Ireland in the year 625, we might be able to infer that a different population had moved there, or that the natives had finally started cultivating plants. At least that's what I'd predict at the end of the second paragraph.

The third paragraph is a specific example, which again seems to prove this prediction correct. Cereal grain pollen in one particular area of Ireland in 400 A.D. allows scientists to make an inference that the people in the area at the time were tilling the soil, a previously unknown fact.

The fourth paragraph is another example. In this case, it's the absence of flax pollen before the eighteenth century which allows scientists to learn that flax was not cultivated in Ireland before that time, contrary to scientists' earlier predictions.

Things are sounding pretty rosy for pollen record science at this point. What can't this amazing pollen record do? Well, the fifth and final paragraph says "not so fast." The pollen record can sometimes only tell the genus and family of a plant, not the exact species. This is a problem in certain instances, like when uncultivated native plants are indistinguishable from certain cultivated plants.

Summing it all up, we get something like "the pollen record is a promising, if imperfect, new tool for scientists to use when examining the history of a place, as demonstrated by its use in Ireland."

Turning to the questions, I remind myself that most Reading Comprehension questions fall into the Must Be True category from Logical Reasoning. I should expect to have evidence from the passage for each answer I pick.

Be an asshole

I'm taking a very confrontational attitude as I read. I'm interrupting the author, and I'm asking very pointed questions, and, frankly, I'm being a dick. And I'm doing all that *on purpose.* I've found that being an asshole forces me to pay attention to the argument. In real life I'd just politely tune out the author's blathering, but for the next 35 minutes I *have* to pay attention. When I put a chip on my shoulder and ask the author "why are you wasting my time with this?" I put myself in a position where I'm obligated to listen for the response.

QUESTION 23:

Which one of the following most accurately expresses the main point of the passage?

A) Analysis of fossilized pollen is a useful means of supplementing and in some cases correcting other sources of information regarding changes in the Irish landscape.
B) Analyses of historical documents, together with pollen evidence, have led to the revision of some previously accepted hypotheses regarding changes in the Irish landscape.
C) Analysis of fossilized pollen has proven to be a valuable tool in the identification of ancient plant species.
D) Analysis of fossilized pollen has provided new evidence that the cultivation of such crops as cereal grains, flax, and madder had a significant impact on the landscape of Ireland.
E) While pollen evidence can sometimes supplement other sources of historical information, its applicability is severely limited, since it cannot be used to identify plant species.

On Main Point questions, it's critical to make a strong prediction. Most of the time, we ought to be able to get pretty close. Again, we're looking for something along to the lines of: "The pollen record is a compelling new tool for historians/scientists, as demonstrated by its use in Ireland."

A) Sure, this looks awfully good and isn't far off of our prediction. This is a strong contender.
B) No, the passage wasn't about analysis of documents. It was about using fossilized pollen to supplement, or even correct, the historical record. This is out.
C) This answer starts off strong, but becomes incorrect when it says "identification of ancient plant species." That's just not the point. The point is fossilized pollen's utility to historians. (Which is a sentence I never thought I'd ever type.)
D) No, "impact on the landscape of Ireland" was never mentioned in the passage. This misses the point.
E) No, "severely limited" was not the point. The general tone of the article was very optimistic about pollen evidence. This answer choice is way too negative.

Our answer is A, because it's the best match for our prediction. We read the passage, we comprehended it, we made a prediction, and the LSAT rewarded us with a correct answer. Feels good, right?

QUESTION 24:

The passage indicates that pollen analyses have provided evidence against which one of the following views?

A) The moldboard plough was introduced into Ireland in the seventh century.
B) In certain parts of County Down, cereal grains were not cultivated to any significant extent before the seventh century.
C) In certain parts of Ireland, cereal grains have been cultivated continuously since the introduction of the moldboard plough.
D) Cereal grain cultivation requires successful tilling of the soil.
E) Cereal grain cultivation began in County Down around 400 A.D.

Since we're asked to find something that pollen analyses has provided evidence against, this one goes in the Must Be False category. We're looking for something that was discussed in the passage, and proven false by the passage. There's really no way to predict this one; we've just got to attack the answer choices.

A) This is a trap. The passage does indicate that some sort of cultivation happened prior to the seventh century, but—and this is the trap part—this didn't have to happen via moldboard plough. For all we know, people were tilling the soil with their fingernails for a few hundred years before they discovered the moldboard plough in the seventh century. This is out.
B) Yep. Pollen analysis has proven that cereal grains were being cultivated in some parts of County Down in A.D. 400, well before the seventh century. This answer has been proven false by the given evidence, so this is going to be our answer. As always, we'll skim C-E just to be sure.
C) No, the passage never said anything about a discontinuation of cereal grain cultivation.
D) No, actually, the presence of cereal grain pollen led scientists to believe that the ground must have been tilled. The fact that cereal grain cultivation requires soil tilling was never questioned.
E) If anything, the pollen record supports this fact; it looks like a Must Be True, when we were looking for a Must Be False.

Our answer is B, because it's the exact opposite of something stated in the passage.

QUESTION 25:

The phrase "documentary record" (lines 20 and 37) primarily refers to

A) documented results of analyses of fossilized pollen
B) the kinds and quantities of fossilized pollen grains preserved in peats and lake muds
C) written and pictorial descriptions by current historians of the events and landscapes of past centuries
D) government and commercial records, maps, and similar documents produced in the past that recorded conditions and events of that time
E) articles, books, and other documents by current historians listing and analyzing all the available evidence regarding a particular historical period

This question goes in the Must Be True category. (You'll find a lot of these in the Reading Comprehension section, generally.) We need to find the closest match to exactly what the passage said. Ideally, the answer will seem boring and obvious: We're looking for something that simply cannot be false, based on the passage.

You may or may not need to refer back to the passage to answer this line reference question. The phrase "documentary record," in both cases, was literally referring to historical documents that provide a record of a certain place. Of course, as the passage pointed out, this record is incomplete and can be supplemented by other historical facts and analyses, such as the pollen record.

A) No, the passage was referring to the historical record generally; the pollen record is discussed as a supplement to this record.
B) No, the pollen record is a different thing.
C) No, the passage was referring to the entire historical record, including specifically old documents; the passage wasn't only talking about things that were written in the present day.
D) Yep, that's pretty much exactly what I was looking for.
E) No, this is wrong for the nearly the same reason as C. The documentary record is the aggregation of all the historical documents from a time; this answer is describing a modern survey of these documents; that's not quite right.

Our answer is D.

QUESTION 26:

The passage indicates that prior to the use of pollen analysis in the study of the history of the Irish landscape, at least some historians believed which one of the following?

A) The Irish landscape had experienced significant flooding during the seventeenth century.
B) Cereal grain was not cultivated anywhere in Ireland until at least the seventh century.
C) The history of the Irish landscape during the sixteenth and seventeenth centuries was well documented.
D) Madder was not used as a dye plant in Ireland until after the eighteenth century.
E) The beginning of flax cultivation in County Down may well have occurred before the eighteenth century.

This is another Must Be True; we're looking for something the passage specifically said that historians believed, prior to the advent of pollen history analysis. Since we already have a firm grasp on what this passage is about, there's not much we can do but go through the answer choices.

A) What? I don't remember anything about flooding.
B) I don't remember the passage saying this either.
C) Not that I recall. The point was that we needed something else to supplement the historical record—the pollen analyses.
D) Nope.
E) Yep, totally. The passage specifically states, in lines 42-44, that some historians surmised that flax was being cultivated in County Down before the eighteenth century.

Our answer is E, because it's stated right there in the passage.

QUESTION 27:

Which one of the following most accurately describes the relationship between the second paragraph and the final paragraph?

A) The second paragraph proposes a hypothesis for which the final paragraph offers a supporting example.
B) The final paragraph describes a problem that must be solved before the method advocated in the second paragraph can be considered viable.
C) The final paragraph qualifies the claim made in the second paragraph.
D) The second paragraph describes a view against which the author intends to argue, and the final paragraph states the author's argument against that view.
E) The final paragraph offers procedures to supplement the method described in the second paragraph.

I had to refer back to the passage for this one, to remember what was in each of the two paragraphs we're being asked about. I quickly summarized the second passage as "details about how pollen analysis works, and why it seems promising" and the last as "a limitation on pollen analysis, with an example of when it doesn't work." Let's see if we can match both of those simultaneously.

A) No, I don't think the second paragraph is a hypothesis and, anyway, the last paragraph is a limitation, not a supporting example.
B) No, I don't think the last paragraph was describing a problem.
C) Yep. The fifth paragraph is qualifying, i.e. limiting, the promising claim at the end of the second paragraph.
D) No, the author definitely doesn't argue against the second paragraph.
E) No, I don't think the fourth paragraph is offering procedures.

Our answer is C, because it's the best description of what's happening in the second and fifth paragraphs.

Tips For Future Study

If you've come this far, you know 80 percent of everything you'll ever need to know about the LSAT. But you probably want to know more, and you definitely need practice *applying* what you know. Here are some quick tips for the next step:

GET YOUR HANDS ON A BUNCH OF OLD TESTS.
If you want to improve your LSAT score, you need to work on REAL LSAT QUESTIONS. Sorry for shouting, but this is non-negotiable. The Law School Admission Council has released five books (with a sixth out in October 2017) in the "10 Actual Official LSAT" series. Find the two most recent books and buy them. If you have time to do more, work backward into the previous volumes as well. But at a minimum, you're simply not prepared if you haven't done the tests in the two most recent volumes. These are the primary texts that I use in my classes and with my tutoring students. Study the real thing. It's worth it.

Another note along these lines: Practice first. I'm always shocked when I speak with a student who has been "studying" for weeks, or even months, but has yet to take their first real practice test. This is a tragic error. If you're not doing real, timed LSAT tests, then you're not doing the LSAT at all. It's like reading book after book about Bicycle Riding Theory without actually getting on a bike. It's a waste of time! The LSAT can be understood largely via common sense, so don't confuse yourself with a bunch of unnecessary trademarked jargon. Start with the actual tests, and let the results show you which areas you need help with.

REVIEW YOUR MISTAKES AND GUESSES.
I have seen so many students blasting through practice test after practice test without thoroughly reviewing their mistakes. This is like practicing free throws without looking to see whether they're going in. Every one of your mistakes is a golden opportunity to learn!

When you miss a question, you need to get ruthless about figuring out exactly what you did wrong. Why did you choose the answer you chose? Why did you not choose the correct answer? Did you understand the argument? Did you understand the question type? Do you frequently miss questions of this type? Also review any question where you guessed—if you narrowed it down to a 50/50 and guessed correctly, you still need to review this question and figure out why the credited answer was better than the second-best answer.

GET YOURSELF A STUDY PARTNER.
Classes and private tutors are amazing, if you can afford one. But a study partner is free, and you should try to get one whether or not you have a paid expert. When I was preparing, my study partner and I met once a week for coffee to review a test that we had each attempted on our own. Sometimes you won't know the answer, and your study partner can explain it to you. Sometimes you'll know the answer, and explain it to your partner. Teaching is the very best way to learn! In some ways, this might be better than working with a tutor.

As a general rule, when you're self-studying, don't take too long reviewing any one question. Give it 5-10 minutes, max, and assemble a list of questions you don't understand. Bring this list to a tutor or study partner, and see if they can help you figure them out.

TURN YOUR WEAKNESSES INTO STRENGTHS.

Do not make the tragic mistake of avoiding your weaknesses! Most students start off with a huge deficit in Logic Games, but this is the most learnable section of the test. If you avoid your weakness in Games, you are missing your best opportunity to *quickly* improve. Start with whichever section you currently suck at the most. Work on it every day until you don't suck at it so much. Then move on to your new weakest section.

PRACTICE, PRACTICE, PRACTICE.

There really aren't that many techniques to master, but you're going to need to put in a lot of reps before you know which technique applies on which question. If you liked this book, you'd probably benefit from my other books as well. *Cheating the LSAT*, *Breaking the LSAT*, and *Exposing the LSAT* each take you step-by-step through an entire recent LSAT test. This is exactly what I do in each one of my classroom courses, and I've written the books to work like a whole course wrapped up into one volume. Another one of my books, *Disrespecting the LSAT*, is an encyclopedia focused solely on Logical Reasoning, and if you're one of the folks with a Logic Games weakness, my newest book, *The Logic Games Playbook*, will definitely help you out.

START NOW, AND DO A LITTLE BIT EVERY DAY.

You won't be ready for swimsuit season if you start doing pushups on June 1. But if you start doing pushups in January, you'll have a hell of a lot of pushups under your belt by the time your first pool party comes around. Rather than trying to cram all your studies in at the last minute, keep it civilized by starting early and doing a tiny bit every day.

I recommend the same basic "study plan" for just about everybody. Do one 35-minute section of a real LSAT every single day, then thoroughly review your mistakes. This should take about an hour in total. Maybe some days you'll find time to do more than one section, but even if you don't, one section a day is enough to make major progress if you do it for three months or more.

MAXIMIZE STUDY TIME WITH MODERN TECH.

Every time I schedule a Skype tutoring session, or refer a Thinking LSAT Podcast listener to my free online class, I get butterflies for technology. Yup, I'm a nerd. But the benefits really are amazing, so definitely avail yourself of the dizzying spectrum of resources available online.

Meet with your study partner via Skype instead of driving across town, giving yourself that much more time to study. Listen to my free LSAT podcast (thinkinglsat. com) while working out or commuting. If you decide to do an online LSAT class, you'll find that it's cheaper than an in-person class and you can increase your LSAT score before work, at lunch, even in your pajamas. Raise your point-increase-per-hour by maxing out on tech.

KEEP IN TOUCH!

As I said at the beginning of the book, I am always here to help. If something is puzzling you, I might be able to keep you from banging your head against the wall. I'm available at **nathan@foxlsat.com** and **415-518-0630**. I know that the LSAT, and law school applications generally, can be a daunting and mystifying experience. I sincerely hope you'll reach out for help.

A Few Details on Law School Applications

The process of applying to law schools isn't a closely guarded mystery. It's a lot like applying to college, with an application, recommendations, transcripts and a writing sample. But there are a few bureaucratic details that you'll have to handle along the way.

You'll need to register for the LSAC's Credential Assembly Service (CAS) before you can officially request law school letters of recommendation and transcripts. The CAS has very particular procedures for making these requests; you'll trigger the requests via the CAS website, and the recommendations and transcripts must then be returned to the CAS without you ever touching them. So you may as well go ahead and register for the service now. (Like most things to do with law school, there's a fee, but the LSAT, the CAS, and most law school applications can be free for those who qualify for the LSAC fee waiver.) Once you're registered for the CAS, you can request transcripts immediately.

It's a good idea to give the folks who will be writing your letters of recommendation a warning before triggering the official CAS request. Get the ball rolling with either an email or a phone call. It's a nice touch to say something like, "I'm not asking you now, but I'm applying to law school this fall and I'm asking if, in the near future, you'd be willing to write a letter of recommendation." This approach shows that you are professional, proactive, and respectful of the recommender's time—which might very well lead to a more positive (and timely) recommendation.

Finally, even if you haven't yet finalized the list of schools to which you will be applying, I recommend that you start an application for at least one or two schools that you're sure you will apply to once applications are open. Obviously you won't submit these applications until you have an LSAT score you're happy with, but in the meantime you can at least start looking at the kinds of questions that will be asked. For example, you can see what type of prompts schools use for the personal statement, and what kinds of diversity statements and other addenda you'll need to draft. Don't half-ass the writing samples—a big part of being a lawyer is writing, so you might as well get used to it.

Studying for the LSAT must remain your number one priority, since your LSAT score is the primary determinant of both where you'll get in and how much, if any, scholarship money you'll be offered. But when you're out of gas on LSAT studying, and it doesn't feel like anything is sinking in, this is a great time to start ticking off some boxes on your law school applications. These things take time, so it's better to start now.

Acknowledgments (with a teensy little request)

My business, including my books, would not exist if not for the power of Internet reviews. The only way a student ever hears about me is from another student, either in a classroom or on the web. Telling a friend is great, but when you write a review you tell the entire world.

If you benefited from this book, and if you want to help my little business compete against the behemoth test prep companies and their giant advertising budgets, the single most awesome thing you can do is go on Amazon, Yelp, or whatever today's hot social network might be, and write your honest opinion. It will take you ten minutes, and I will be eternally grateful. Thank you so much for your support.

NEED A LITTLE HELP?
Call me.

I'M HERE TO HELP

Stop banging your head against the wall!
The LSAT and law school admissions aren't as
mind-boggling as you think. If you're struggling
with a certain question type, or you're confused
by the whole "sufficient vs. necessary" thing, or
you want to know how to negotiate for law school
scholarships, please let me help! I'm a nerd about
this stuff, and I love to show students how easy it
can be. Email me any time at **nathan@foxlsat.com**,
or just pick up the phone. I'm generally available to
talk between 10 am and 6 pm PST.

STUDY SMARTER

Join me and my co-host of the Thinking LSAT
podcast, Ben Olson, for access to our killer
LSAT explanations at LSATDemon.com. The
Demon learns from your mistakes and gives you
questions targeted toward your weaknesses,
at your ideal difficulty level. Do timed sections
at 35, 53, or 70 minutes. Attend full proctored
practice tests with other Demon users around
the world. And do it all from anywhere—on your
phone, tablet, or computer.

Do a 7-day free trial today at **www.LSATdemon.com.**

No confusing jargon, no pulled punches, no bullshit.
LSAT made simple.

Manufactured by Amazon.ca
Bolton, ON

35336566R00055